Standards Matter

STANDARDS MATTER

The Why and What of Common Core State Standards in Reading and Writing

KATHERINE SCHEIDLER

NEWSOUTH BOOKS
Montgomery

NewSouth Books
105 S. Court Street
Montgomery, AL 36104

Copyright © 2015 by Katherine Scheidler
All rights reserved under International and Pan-American Copyright Conventions.
Published in the United States by NewSouth Books, a division of NewSouth, Inc.,
Montgomery, Alabama.

Publisher's Cataloging-in-Publication data

Scheidler, Katherine
Standards matter : the why and what of Common Core State Standards in
reading and writing / Katherine Scheidler
p. cm.
Includes index.

ISBN 978-1-60306-376-0 (paperback)
ISBN 978-1-60306-377-7 (ebook)

1. Education—Standards—United States. 2. Academic achievement—United States.
I. Title.

2014956941

Printed in the United States of America
by BR Printers

To Peter

Contents

Preface / ix

Chapter One
Why Standards Matter / 3

Chapter Two
Happy Living in a Standards-Based World / 17

Chapter Three
Seeing What Our Students Can Do: One Model / 28

Chapter Four
How Did We Get Here? / 37

Chapter Five
Developing High-Level Reading Ability / 41

Chapter Six
The Reading Standards / 50

Chapter Seven
The Reading Standards Part II: Craft and Structure / 54

Chapter Eight
The Reading Standards III: Knowledge and Ideas / 57

Chapter Nine
Common Core Writing Standards / 62

Chapter Ten
A Sea Change / 67

About the Author / 77

Index / 78

Preface

Common Core State Standards with National Tests

The Background

In 1983 the National Commission on Excellence in Education reported in *A Nation at Risk* on the "rising tide of mediocrity" believed to be found nationally in U.S. schools, a finding spurred on in part by Japan's dramatic growth in economic power and a national concern that other countries were outperforming the United States in education achievement. In the education field, we were asked to look at Japanese schools to take lessons from their model of education.

A Nation at Risk stimulated discussion in the policy world of how to improve America's schools. At a 1989 National Governors Conference, the governors unanimously agreed to work with the White House on national performance standards aimed at developing a high level of education.

Individual states developed different standards and measures of success, with state tests varying in level of difficulty.

In 2002, the George W. Bush administration received bipartisan congressional approval for the "No Child Left Behind" federal legislation, which replaced the toothless Elementary and Secondary Education Act of 1965. NCLB tightened its grip on education nationally with the goal of all students reaching the level of Proficient on the varied state standards on state tests by 2014. President Bush signed the No Child Left Behind Act into law January 8, 2002.

NCLB initiated standards-based education reform on the premise that setting high standards and establishing measurable goals can improve individual student outcomes in education. The ambitious goal of all students attaining Proficient level or above in 12 years, a goal that would have overcome decades of lack of success in this area, was not achieved.

But NCLB federal legislation did impact the development and implementation of state standards and state tests that guide and assess teaching and learning. This constituted a major shift in how public schools worked and was a highly controversial program of top-down state regulation, but it was gradually accepted and implemented as part of the way of life for schools. Not surprisingly, in the end, school system test scores correlated by and large with demographics. The standards and tests promoted more common education, but on the larger scale, traditionally lower-performing student groups continued to score lower than middle-class white students, and often below Proficient. Reauthorization of NCLB languished after 2011.

With lack of congressional agreement on what policy to take next, and finding some schools pushing back on freedom to teach, Congress could not decide on next steps.

New standards for national commonality, intended to succeed NCLB's earlier state standards, were then independently developed outside of Congress and the Administration. In 2009 the National Governors Association convened a team to write new learning standards, which were released on June 2, 2010. These Standards are copyrighted by the National Governors Association Center for Best Practices and the Council for Chief State School Officers and are licensed to State Departments of Education. Over forty states voluntarily adopted this new set of common high-level Standards, the Common Core State Standards in literacy and mathematics.

After the failure on the NCLB goal of all students attaining Proficient as measured by state tests, the Common Core Standards were to support a less ambitious goal, that of narrowing by half by 2016–17 the achievement gap between middle-class white students and the low-income, racial minority groups, English language learners, and special education groups.

In addition, with Congress unable to agree on follow-up policy to No Child Left Behind, the Obama administration developed and announced another ambitious federal education program called "Race to the Top." States were asked to apply to join this program of promoting student learning growth, and selected states obtained federal funds for three years starting in the 2010–11 school year. Fifteen states were accepted for this ambitious program with more regulations.

New, more challenging national tests on Common Core State Standards were scheduled to begin in 2015.

In the wake of the contentiousness that has arisen over Common Core State Standards, this book aims to provide a concise overview of the issues, from the perspective of an education insider who has decades of work and study in urban and suburban districts as a teacher, school system administrator, and teacher of teachers.

We haven't informed the public well on what these Standards are. I address here what I recognize as confusion or misinformation about Common Core State Standards and provide the rationale for the Standards. I explore in depth just two areas, examples of the reading and writing Common Core Standards.*

I believe that we in education haven't explained well the "why" of Standards learning, which I see from the perspective of my own and others' classrooms, my years of teaching in an urban school, from study of education research, from the view of the school system central office, and the parent perspective.

I attempt to explain how Standards learning is helping our public schools nationally with the expectation of a high quality of education for all students.

What we don't know can hurt us.

---

* To distinguish standards references, we use "Common Core State Standards" references with a capital "S"; references to standards in general and from earlier periods are used with lowercase "s."

Standards Matter

Chapter One

WHY STANDARDS MATTER

THE BIG PICTURE

Few want to say that our schools are failing. And indeed, many schools are not. But we're not effective enough with too many students. District and school reports continue to show on the whole that white middle-class students perform higher than other racial groups and low-income students on state and other varied tests. Special needs students can also improve. Certainly we must also help with English language learners; it's their right, too.

It's not that teachers aren't trying. The system and the public as a whole must more fully support this growth in education expectations. With the national Common Core State Standards learning guidelines, voluntarily adopted by states, and the U.S. Department of Education Race to the Top goal of narrowing the achievement gap, we can and must work to help all students learn at the levels of students coming from more advantaged homes. Public schools are intended to educate all students. Our students who have been consistently left behind are the students who most depend on teachers to learn.

New learning Standards and tests ratchet up expectations nationally. Common Core State Standards are more complex and high level than standards of the past decade. The 15 states that adopted the federal Race to the Top program also have Educator Evaluation criteria that in part includes teachers' student test scores over a period of time to show Standards learning growth. A teacher makes a difference. Administrators and often parents have long known which teachers are teaching well and which may need more supports; this isn't new. Now we work with teachers to help them become stronger. We all can become better at what we do. We have the tools that can help students learn. Now teachers are asked to use these tools, and districts must provide the supports needed.

Test Critics

Overwhelmed school administrators and teachers often chafe at national tests, accountability, and regulations. Parents who don't fully understand the Common Core Standards fear their children won't get a good education. Academics criticize the state tests as too narrow, constraining, and simple-minded an approach to assess student learning. Teachers, principals, and district managers are already busy enough with simply maintaining schools in conformance with other state and federal regulations. Moreover, every school has its hundreds of students sitting in their classrooms, there for learning. Education reform is often referred to as changing the tires while the car is moving.

New Types of Tests

Critics complain of too much "standardized testing." But these newer tests are not the old, secret standardized tests of what students already know. Originally intended to assess what students know in order to help them, the IQ tests of the 1960s and earlier instead came to be used to see how smart a student is, to nail down learning capability. A low-IQ student was labeled as not very smart and we had to lower materials, expectations, and learning levels, hindering growth.

Today we know all students can be helped to learn. There are different kinds of tests for different purposes. Today's standards tests are intended to let educators see the standards to learn, then assess to see if students have learned them. Is this teaching for the test? Yes, in a good way, to set out learning goals, help students learn the needed areas, then assess student learning on these understandings.

Today's state standards tests are a different type of test. They're not standardized tests. State learning assessments now are "criterion-referenced" tests in which teachers, students, and parents are provided the test information of the standards in advance and promote this learning, and then assess growth on the outside state tests. Students are tested on criteria provided in advance. These criteria, or standards, are used to develop student learning, then check to see if students did learn.

Expected test items can be easily accessed on the internet by teachers and students and parents, as has long been done with Advanced Placement tests for higher-achieving students. AP teachers teach to the test. Students learn. An AP teacher eagerly anticipates her students' AP test scores, and calculates how well her students have done. The teacher delves into the test scores. Which students scored highest? What's the average score this year? Are there surprises in score results? We can't help but enjoy the teacher's self-congratulation and delight with her students' high AP test scores. AP teachers take pride in their students' scores. The teacher knows the impact she has on her students. The teacher strives to do better, to have higher test scores the next year. The teacher knows her work counts for her students' results.

Do we hear complaints from parents on this, that the teacher is teaching to the test? The teachers use earlier practice tests to help students get acquainted with the test format. Often teachers attend annual AP institutes to continue to learn on their own. The teacher knows the growth comes mostly from the classroom instruction, the teaching and learning. Why not have such a system for all students?

Similarly, we've long had the high-stakes Scholastic Aptitude Test (SAT) with the score results factored into college acceptance. We have a multitude of SAT "prep" courses and materials and individual tutoring.

Why deny this learning of Common Core Standards higher level reading, writing and math learning as goals for more struggling students? Why deny teaching them skills and understandings that our higher-achieving students may know and learn in their classes?

Standardized Tests Versus "Criterion-Referenced Tests" to Set Out Learning Goals and Teach for the Test

Critics say "bubble tests"—multiple choice test questions—are not sufficient, though they have long been used as learning measures on AP and SAT tests and the Graduate Record Exam (GRE) tests for graduate school acceptance. SAT, AP, and GRE test-prep books are bestsellers. Prospective law and medical students cram for the profession's college admissions test. Students who can afford the often high cost of SAT course prep have long practiced and had tutors for the SAT test, to bump up their scores.

Current Standards assessments are the best type of test we have to determine learning of huge numbers of students. Further, Common Core Standards tests require more and varied types of writing, scored not by machine but by humans trained well to assess writing. We've had decades of practice in how to assess writing in a common, reliable way, practice developed and refined for national tests by the Educational Testing Service (ETS), based in Princeton, New Jersey. The test readers are dismissed if results are not found to be reliable or what is expected of each reader.

Good Tests

We can and must focus on higher levels of learning, and for all students. Tests used to measure learning on Standards are a good measure of our success. We must ensure that all students are taught the same high-level reading, writing, and math skills and understandings. The sophisticated testing companies are using the tools they've refined over the years to make the tests as valid (testing what is intended to be tested) and reliable (consistent over time) assessments of learning as possible. The tests don't lie. Multiple choice guessing won't cut it.

Helping All Students

Are the national tests for Standards fair? One of my urban African American students, Charity, fell in love with Alice Walker's writing. Charity read all of Walker's books for a class project. But Charity was unable to get the SAT test score—at the time heavily weighted toward vocabulary—to qualify for a scholarship for the college Alice Walker had attended, Atlanta's Spelman College. Spelman is a historically black college for women, sister school of the elite all-male Morehouse College.

Charity was brilliant, articulate, a sensitive reader, and a powerful, skillful writer. But her neighborhood life hadn't given her the opportunity to learn the vocabulary then needed for the SAT test, which had been working on the old test assumption that smart people know more-challenging vocabulary. Not true. Today ETS recognizes that vocabulary knowledge is discriminating and has eliminated much vocabulary testing.

Children of lower-income homes can learn challenging vocabulary. Intelligence is malleable. This is the assumption of Common Core State Standards and the national tests of this learning. The Standards goal is to help all students grow, and it sets a magnificent framework for this growth.

Charity ultimately went to a different black college. This brilliant young woman was denied the high-quality education that Spelman College could have given her. The K–12 public school system did not serve Charity well. Busy as a teacher with over a hundred needy students myself, I deeply regret that I didn't drop my dozens of other pressing needs and help Charity learn the vocabulary she needed for the SAT test. This development of vocabulary ability was a heavy emphasis on our state's No Child Left Behind tests of the 1990s, and it is also emphasized on Current Common Core State Standards tests, beginning in the early elementary grades.

However, today's national tests focus on use of text context clues to determine word meaning, an ability that helps develop vocabulary understanding. Old tests simply tested word meaning.

Building vocabulary increases reading comprehension and expands ideas and expression. Limited vocabulary limits precise expression and reading comprehension. I tell the teachers with whom I work on teaching Common Core Standards to use their local sports pages, brief appealing poems, song lyrics with some challenging words—whatever works—to help students learn how to discern word meaning from context.

When I was teaching English, I asked my urban students to put away their newspapers. These young men were reading the football and basketball articles of the state newspaper at the level of critical analysis, sailing through the colorful and sophisticated vocabulary and figurative language with total comprehension, learning how to read complex text. Common Core State Standards specifically state that they don't restrict teachers in their teaching methods. The Standards frameworks don't dictate *how* to teach the Standards, freeing teachers to do what works. I should have seized the chance to use what students were passionately reading to develop their reading and writing ability, instead of taking them to more remote, deadly reading that killed rather than instilled ability.

Start Where the Child Is

Importantly, Common Core Standards don't mandate *how* a teacher should teach. Looking back at all the students I feel I left behind in my own teaching, and knowing now what Common Core Standards ask of us, I know I should have used what was close to the students' interest to begin teaching the skills needed, then move to more-challenging reading and writing. As our beloved NFL quarterback, with his open self-criticism and humility, states after a crushing loss, "They don't send me out there just to follow rules. They send me out there to be smart." Common Core Standards ask teachers to understand the goal, the bigger picture, and to be smart in how one teaches the students in front of them who need their help.

Perhaps Charity and others are doing fine now. I hope her wonderful personal qualities, love of learning, and enthusiasm have served her well. As teachers, most often we never know. I only know I didn't serve many of my needy students as well as I might have. To be honest, there wasn't outside pressure for helping all students. We need this stimulus.

This is the goal of Common Core State Standards and state and national tests, to set us straight as educational institutions fair to all. The aim is not to harass or over-burden teachers, or drive them from the profession, but to provide schools and teachers with the same guides for all students, and to support teachers in this work.

Equity and Justice

The federal goal of narrowing the achievement gap between the "haves" and "have-nots" speaks to our sense of fairness. Moreover, Standards guides provide the grade-level expectations, test companies have posted test question samples, publishers are providing resource materials, and the talk of the profession is an emphasis on collaboration, not isolation. Internet resources abound, especially now that Standards are common nationally. Teachers are taking advantage of what they can find that works for them and meets their needs for their students. Teachers share with one another.

The "lone ranger" independent teacher doesn't help in the huge effort the rigorous Standards and tests require of schools. Sharing practice and discussing successes and failures in a trusting, supportive environment wins.

The earlier toxic environment of competition, discussing travel ("escape") plans instead of lesson plans, not being a good colleague, and the school culture of complaint don't serve teachers or students well.

No longer are teachers to close their classroom doors to sink or swim, but to work in concert with colleagues to figure out better ways of teaching. School has changed for the better from the private practice of the 1950s. Now I see teachers eager for new and better ideas. Now I see teachers not simply getting through the school day, with the one thing teachers could agree on—that payday is good.

Now I see teachers wanting to be the best teacher he or she can be, for one's students. And teachers know that one measure is when they see their own students' state test scores at the end of the school year. When teachers teach the Standards learning in such a way that all students learn, this is reflected in the test scores. Does a football player measure himself on how well he alone played a game? If he did, he wouldn't last long. It's teamwork, constant new individual and group learning to face the next new challenge, always striving to improve, and in the end, the final score, the test result, that measures success. This energy, goal-driven work, and teamwork are what I now see with teachers across the country. And this vast change in school culture is in large part thanks to Common Core State Standards and state tests. This can't be all bad.

Raising the Bar, for All

When we hear of a special needs child not learning to read in school, when we have absenteeism and student behavior problems, look at percentages of students not attending college, or worse, not graduating from high school, see students floundering after college in what seems a jobless world today for many, we wonder. Can we do better? Can nonlearners become learners? We have students doing exceptionally well, students doing adequately, and a significant group not succeeding at a Proficient level of math understanding or reading and writing at high levels. We know those students. They may well be self-defeating in school behavior. We see them in classrooms. Can we turn these students around? Research and experience inform us we can.

Paradigm Shift

How do we change to serve all students well in learning growth?

As we continuously hear of and read derision and concerns on "testing" children in our schools today, an old theory of change is worth giving a closer look. The thoughts behind the concept of a paradigm shift shed light on the issue and enlighten us with ways of understanding of how to help schools address new learning expectations. This concept of paradigm shift is much more than a cliché.

The old system taught—and some classrooms still teach—to the better students. Research studies prior to the 1990s show that the one factor of demographics correlates with achievement. "Tell me a student's family income and I'll tell you his SAT score," stated education reformer Ted Sizer in the 1980s.

The high-demographic students from families of relative wealth and education often perform well in school. Their parents read to them at home, support their school work, and attend parent-teacher conferences to hear the good and bad news to learn student needs. "Peter, if you do really well in school this year, I won't bother you at all about this next year," was one "conversation" I had with our son. "Mom, you said that last year," he retaliated. But he did get the message.

As a group, low-income students and children of color do more poorly. Not surprisingly, English language learners—the euphemism for immigrant students with limited English skills—traditionally perform below middle-class white children born in this country. Research and practice show we can help children who need more assistance with learning to move to higher levels.

We can't blame teachers for not assisting students who are not engaged in school, who are impatient and act out their frustrations in class. It hasn't been a requirement of the teachers' job to focus on helping these students. In the past, making it a major focus to seek ways to assist these underperforming students hasn't been recognized or rewarded. But we must understand that many students come to school hungry, sometimes from difficult, chaotic home lives in which survival is the mode of living. Some students simply feel unable to compete—the bar is too high. Hard-to-reach students are created by layers of defensive, at times even belligerent, behavior toward a system in which one feels one can't be successful. These students may well have the potential to excel under the right conditions. National Standards and tests insist that we try.

Marginalized, struggling students exist in all schools. The thinking in school reform for more than 50 years has been to better serve all students. As group, the move to high-level Standards, challenging state tests, student growth, and a relatively more stringent Educator Evaluation system constitute a paradigm shift from earlier years.

The Tsunami

These rules of grade-level Standards learning, state tests, and expected student learning growth set a different focus. It's a tsunami for schools. It's no wonder that we hear and read the waves of criticism. Those who think teaching is easy, apart from Standards learning and accountability, should spend a few weeks in a classroom with over 100 students coming in and out, multiple courses to teach, administrative intrusion, a 12-minute lunch break, the lively, even manic and distracted world of adolescents, and barely time to speak with another adult. Administrators are left just trying to steady the ship, let alone steer it. Teaching has rarely been easy.

With Standards learning, many teachers come on board and work to power change, often as individuals. Some do not get on board, and they discourage others. At times these "not going to happen" voices are strident and shut down forward movement. Others, who may be able to meet the new expectations, feel lost, abandon ship and leave the profession. It's perhaps hardest for veteran teachers who were trained and have long experience under the earlier "factory system" of teacher-centered, not student-centered, teaching. The shift in thinking and practice is accomplished by many. For others, the shift is hard. It's different from past practice. It helps tremendously if we can understand the big-picture need.

Bright Lights of Success

The marvel is that we see efforts made and success with high-level Standards and challenging tests, but not by magic. These changes come from devoted, sincere attempts by administrators and teachers. Successful pockets of reforms that preceded current guidelines are well documented on small-scale levels. Reports show that school can change students, save lives. Some charter schools work with the most challenging students, and, dependent upon strong test scores for survival, bring children along with smaller numbers of students and a strong focus on learning. These schools go beyond just teaching for the test, go for high-quality learning, and accomplish what can't be done in larger public schools. Or can it?

In the 1990s, state standards, state tests, and accountability expectations under No Child Left Behind which were at first shocking eventually became accepted and integrated into school life. Scattered examples of high-quality, focused education have produced significant gains in learning as seen both subjectively in classrooms and on outside objective state test score results.

Many states and districts sailed through that NCLB decade fairly smoothly. Many students learned more during this past period. Special Education learning has been transformed with the higher expectations that include students with learning disabilities; with the dedicated devotion of teachers, these students are now accomplishing what wasn't expected earlier.

NARROWING THE ACHIEVEMENT GAP

It's a cliché to state that the mill and factory jobs for lower-achieving students of the 1950s no longer exist. Our nice filling station attendants who pumped gas into our cars no longer have jobs. Bookstores have been replaced by on-line purchases. Robo-calls have replaced telemarketers. Even software development has been outsourced to India and China. Technology has killed thousands of jobs while young obsessive tech geniuses have become millionaires. Without reading, writing, and math skill and critical thinking ability, what future exists for our students? And how can we think of not helping all students as well as we can? This is a moral issue.

However, after 10 years of clear standards for all students in math and literacy, we're still left with the achievement gap. Our low-income students, children of color, English language learners, and special needs students, as groups, still have not attained the level of Proficient and score below middle-class white students on tests in which what will be tested is prominently seen in advance. Cultural patterns still trump school in the big picture.

The Common Core State Standards goal is to narrow the achievement gap while also raising the bar with higher level, more rigorous national Common Core Standards. This speaks to our internal sense of fairness. It's why we became teachers, to help children.

We now have a fairer accountability system that looks at student growth: English language learners and special education, low-income, and students of color are not required to reach Proficient, but to show growth. Some still call this learning-growth expectation unfair. Actually, it's the status quo that's unfair to our students.

We can't say that school people aren't trying. But even high-performing school districts, in high-demographic communities, aren't always making the progress with traditionally underperforming groups that we want to see. Having high expectations for all is assailed by many, but it may be a lofty but doable goal. We know well the challenges but have to keep trying. It's well worth the effort. We've seen underperforming students learn to succeed. We can't write off any student. This requires a new school focus.

Opening the Doors to Learning

Classroom practice is no longer private practice. Public test scores reflect the quality of teaching on standards learning. Certainly, teachers may have more-challenging students one year, or for two years, which is reflected in scores, but over time in a multi-year pattern teachers are expected to show strong performance. Teachers who consistently have strong test scores are noticed. The few teachers who don't show learning on state tests are urged to seek out means of improvement. The schools and districts must assist these teachers. This is a new way for schools and districts to work. Districts must help pick up this responsibility.

We have the tools.

Common Core State Standards are at our fingertips, with multiple databases of the Standards available on the internet. Of course there's an iPad Common Core Standards app. A teacher can easily access the version of the Standards for his or her grade level. The grade-level mastery level Standards can be used to help a special needs student learn and grow.

In addition, the past decade has brought to schools a multitude of means of supporting struggling learners. Such information also is easily accessed on the internet. We have the tools of differentiated learning, varied learning strategies, self-paced software applications for learning, varied materials and teaching ideas, ease of student research via the internet, and in many schools a culture that supports collaboration, with teachers helping and learning from others.

A Change in Beliefs and Action

This period of high-level Standards and rigorous assessment expects student growth. The growth is a goal in which earlier reform efforts have failed.

This national experiment of improving the quality of learning for all students requires a paradigm shift in beliefs, actions and skills from earlier years; it will be a greater challenge for some than for others. It's demanding work to move struggling students along in annual growth, with challenging state tests, while constantly seeking practice that will help each child. But this is accomplished in varied settings. Raising the learning level can happen on a national level if we have the will and try.

Standards Aren't New

The good news is that most of the Reading and Writing Standards are familiar to us. They're what I taught my "high level" classes, and that in many cases are still taught to only the higher achieving students. Adopting these Standards for all our students is the challenge. As the grade-level Common Core State Standards become adopted by all teachers, teachers have a ladder to build on each year. Taking the next step up in learning a Standard thereby becomes easier, as the Common Core Standards increase in difficulty each year. Student research—in some schools often only introduced in high school—begins in third grade. This grade-level Standards mastery framework is better than the curriculum anarchy of earlier days, in which teachers had the "freedom" to teach, or not, as they wished. Now the focus is as it should and must be, on helping all students learn at high levels, leveling the playing field so that the child born in poverty may have the same access to a bright future as the child born to affluence, with typically well-educated parents with the resources to provide the home and school supports for learning.

Teachers can independently determine how they teach these skills and understandings, though the more commonality, the better, especially for struggling students.

The Common Core Standards include teachers from science and social studies content areas in teaching the reading and writing skills and understandings, to help support literacy growth. Common learning across the disciplines ensures student growth. Also, with greater literacy understandings students learn the content area more easily; a physics or history text becomes more comprehensible with teaching *how* to read in the science or history class.

What about the Higher-Achieving Students?

The higher-achieving students are those the teachers love to work with. Higher learning standards are always expected of these students who are attuned with school, respond to instruction, engage in learning, and can work beyond class expectations. What teacher doesn't want to push these responsive, eager-to-learn students to higher levels? However, the higher-achieving students also must learn the Common Core Standards to ensure that they master these high-quality key learning areas. Constructing an argument or assessing a writer's argument is essential for every student to learn by following the fine Standards guidelines. The more advanced learner, too, must learn the paraphrasing and precise means of documentation of research information required by the Standards.

Struggling students need special teacher attention. Research shows that higher-achieving students perform better with more open-ended learning and less teacher talk. The implication is that if the teacher steps out of the way, but provides learning guides, high-achieving students can learn at higher levels, independently pushing themselves. One advanced chemistry teacher told me that with one class of five students, he loved that he could just let the students discuss the content area and readings on their own. These are the students who went on to Princeton, CalTech, Harvard. They learned from each other, debating information and issues, challenging one another. Certainly we want this exciting learning for these students also.

"Dumbing Down" Learning

In the following chapters that explain the Standards, the reader will see that by providing a common framework, learning is increased, not limited. Because Standards learning is high level, it raises the bar for every student, including higher-achieving students. No one can argue or deny that the Standards are the best practice in the content area. When students learn the Standards, the teacher is free to add additional learning. The risk is that with total teacher freedom of what to teach, learning may in fact be "dumbed down."

Explaining the Standards

When I hear Standards learning being denigrated, I often wonder if the complaining individual knows what the Standards are. This book aims to help inform the reader of the rationale behind national high-level Common Core State Standards and national tests and also what the Reading and Writing Common Core Standards are. The goal is to smooth the reader's way toward better understanding of Common Core Standards learning, to help the reader see why these Standards are good for everyone, and that they are needed to keep our country strong.

We need all of our young people to have the highest quality of education to keep our country at its best nationally. Common Core State Standards and tests help ensure this goal can be reached.

Chapter Two

Happy Living in a Standards-Based World

I have to say that one positive thing about teaching in an urban high school for over 20 years is that there was rarely a dull moment. Periodically school change was thrust upon us.

On the flip side, those lively times were stress-filled, anxiety-producing, and created tensions among fellow teachers. Yet through all the discussion, dissension, and striving, we teachers learned and grew. And despite the challenges, we were all basically committed to our students' learning. But tensions arose from the different ways in which teachers taught, and what we taught. The students were the victims in the sense that even teachers of the same courses taught not only in quite different ways but also taught different content.

The fact that I remained in this teaching position as long as I did was pretty much inertia.

My school was conveniently right across the street from our son's fine private Quaker School, with its small classes, where the teachers were saints who spent the time with and showed children the respect to help them grow into well-educated, ethical, intelligent, knowledgeable, successful go-getters. These special teachers pushed students while being infinitely patient, fun, supportive model adults. Each child was treated well. These students went on to elite colleges.

Across the street at Hope High School, things were different. I had students who were recent immigrants and spoke little English; reading for them was impossible so they faked it, copying their writing directly from text. In speech, these new arrivals picked up the words they heard from other students, feigning and improvising communication, often using street language. I had gifted white students who were teased by classmates;

brilliant, articulate Hispanic girls who were leaders just by virtue of who they were, and students of color passionate about ideas. We also had students who today might well be assessed with ADHD (Attention Deficit and Hyperactivity Disorder) and were ill served in a large urban school at that time. Our high percentage of students now termed "English Language Learners" often expressed their frustrations by acting out.

Learning was variable even for native students. This was certainly so for students who moved in from another district or another state—often low-income students who were transient through no fault of their own. Without commonality within a grade level or over the grades, it's no wonder that student achievement was less than proficient. Demographics largely determined what students did or didn't know. Some could read and write when they came into our classes; others couldn't.

Hope High School wasn't always like this. When I first started teaching there right out of Brown University, students were assigned to three set tracks. I was informed by my department head that the top track was to learn literary analysis terms; the classic texts were reserved for this level. The middle track learned from a "teacher-proof" anthology—just go through the book page by page and ask the questions at the end of the passage. The bottom track, I was told, just needed to hear "correct" English usage. My department head told me I should just speak to them in middle-class "proper" English, so they would learn standard language.

I was afraid to meet that class called the "lower level." I imagined a "Blackboard Jungle" with unruly students. It turned out the students were very sweet in this small class, and when encouraged, they had a lot to say that was interesting. An African American student wore dark glasses, giving him what in my naive innocence I saw as a quite sinister, Black Pantherish look. He turned out to be a very nice young man who wore the dark glasses because he had an eye defect.

What I discovered was that these students not only understood our readings, they had strong opinions on the ideas in the text, which they articulated well. They spoke English just fine. Decades later I can still see their faces. The students called the "low level" became the lost students. Though high numbers of students of color were enrolled, few of these students even graduated. Only the top-track students were being prepared for the top colleges.

I talk with people today who bemoan when Hope was a *good* school. What they mean is that it was good for them.

At this time we had the children of the local university professors at our school. The East Side community liked the strict discipline in which students were "counseled out" and expelled. The tracking system served the middle-class white students just fine. The lovely row of cherry trees across the front lawn of the huge building had been planted by the involved East Side parents. Today that row of bright, hopeful blossoming trees is still there, but that East Side community no longer sends its students to Hope; middle-class families have moved to the suburbs or send their children to the private schools. If their finances are tight, their students attend the public exam school.

When I began teaching, school clearly wasn't serving all kids.

Then Hope High School exploded.

My alarmed students informed me before school one spring day that some African American students had come to school with weapons. Acculturated by my veteran colleagues, I vaguely heard but disregarded as just another rumor what they were telling me. I urged the students to go to their classes. Then we heard it. From my classroom on the third floor, it sounded like the first floor blew up. Students charged down the first-floor corridor with long poles, smashing the corridor lights. A rumor went around that one teacher was injured; later the story was only that she was pushed. We shivered at another rumor that someone heard a gunshot. It turned out not to be true. But in the moment, the back door of my classroom was quickly opened and a teacher pushed in her students who had been in the library with its open doors. Chaos reigned. My classroom doors were locked from the outside. No one said anything. No one knew anything. We didn't understand what was happening. We were stunned, clueless.

In the aftermath, our school was closed for two weeks. Our entire faculty and administration met in another building. We talked as a group and tried to make sense of what from then on was simply called "the riot." Slowly the pieces came together. Unlike today's random school attacks by disturbed individuals, this disruption was political. A group of students charged that the system and some teachers were racist. They wanted change.

As a new young teacher, I listened to what was being reported to us and tried to hear them as grievances expressed by our students of color. I also heard and tried to understand the denials of our staff. Some dismissed the event or charged it was instigated by "outsiders." Others tried to address the charges.

Subsequently, we were provided sensitivity sessions, with presentations and meetings in small groups. We threw out our old leveled curriculum and developed a quarterly course change in which we could create our own mini-courses on any topic. A student could choose any course. There was no leveling of courses or students. This was an attempt to respond to the charges against discriminatory student tracking. Little had been expected of or provided to our minority students. High-level district and school administrators, to their credit, had heard and responded to the charge of discrimination. Our new untracked mini-courses, leveled only by student interest, were intended to better serve all students.

Our English department rose to the occasion. Our heroic, gray-haired distinguished department chair held open discussions. He was infinitely patient. He listened to us, and he led. It takes a respected school leader to promote change from within. We met often, at times at a teacher's home. This was different from the earlier lack of real communication. We changed our teaching and what we taught in an attempt to speak to students. This was stressful, fun, and a lot of work, creating many new courses. We all were engaged, that was for sure. Veteran teachers put aside treasured classic texts—the formerly required *Silas Marner* types—to try to fit this new world.

This major change was especially unsettling to our veteran teachers. Their formerly set world was shaken, their belief systems challenged. Over time, standards slipped.

Times changed, again. The *back to basics* movement arrived. Our quarterly courses were eliminated. The rotating schedule, which gave each class a chance to meet at a better time of day, was dropped. A boring set schedule of teaching five classes a day promoted ennui, not enthusiasm. Helping individuals was not in the program. School became dull for me, so I can imagine what it was like for our students. There had to be something else.

Yet veteran teachers were happy. "The pendulum has swung back," one delightedly announced in the faculty lunchroom. We reverted to the old, leveled, factory model, which short-changed struggling students. Even with the dramatic impact we had experienced from the revolt of students and their supporters, we saw how easily school reverts back to the old ways without continued leadership. And our upper echelon of students was now long gone, a result of white flight accelerated by the earlier disruption.

This was the pre-data era. We had only our opinions to prove whether or not our changes had worked for students.

We returned to the old stratified classes. The strong pull back to the old system was dictated by the beleaguered top administrators. They were of the older generation, and the traditional way was what they knew. Ostensibly the return to the old system resulted in a better, more stable environment. But except in management, school now lacked focus and wasn't working in the sense of learning. Again, demographics determined achievement and destiny. And now the demographics were 85 percent low-income, children of color, English language learners, and special needs students. Other students had left our East Side school for the suburbs, private schools, or the city exam school. We were in a downward spiral; discipline issues increased.

Then came Ted Sizer, Ivy Leaguer, "Boy Dean" of the Harvard Graduate School of Education and former headmaster of Phillips Academy. Sizer became chairman of the nearby Brown University Education Department, just a few blocks down the street from our school.

Sizer knew the school research. Professor Jeannie Oakes of UC Berkeley had studied schools and found that only the top-track students were getting the privileged information that prepared them for college. Primarily it was only those students in the top-level courses who acquired the study habits, strong reading and writing skills, academic learning, terminology, and behaviors that would serve them well in college and the modern workplace. The traditional school had tracked the students who would become factory workers versus the elite who were to attend college. The school structure was not changing student achievement across these lines. Sizer bravely confronted the reality that public schools for the most part weren't making a difference. Not everyone wanted to hear this.

Sizer brought education researcher James Coleman to speak at Brown. Coleman's large-scale quantitative study showed that of all the "in-puts"—teacher degrees, teacher salaries, media resources, class size, per pupil expenditure—the one data piece that correlated with high achievement was demographics. Sizer, himself a product of private boarding schools, popularized the understanding that schools were doing a disservice to struggling students. He made it real to school people. As a teacher, it took me a long time to understand this perspective.

Magically, and marking as profound a change as our "riot" that had turned our school and our world upside down, our new, younger principal befriended Sizer, who spoke to our faculty. To my surprise, our faculty voted by 85 percent to have a program in our school that would be different. I had been on a leave that year, ready to resign from a sense of lack of accomplishment in my teaching. But I heard about this change. Returning to "Hope"—the building and the ambition—I was asked to pick up the first full year of ninth-grade students in this new program.

I would be co-teaching with a social studies teacher in one large space. No longer isolated in our own classrooms, we conferred on our cross-discipline courses and on our students. Talking with a colleague helped immensely. But, long separated from speaking with other teachers in our former sink or swim world when there was no time for teacher collaboration, we lacked full collegiality. As a group, we found collaboration hard. Today, in one of Sizer's great legacies which he termed "the conversation," teachers talk. Now we've moved from the conversation to regulation. Collaboration helps and is now prized in schools.

Students changed in our new program. Our teaching schedule had two long block classes that alternated day to day, then lunch, a team meeting period to confer with teachers sharing the same 100 students, and a private "prep" period. This was a dream schedule. Tracking was eliminated. I taught just ninth-grade English, the same course for all, modifying as needed for the particular students. Struggling students became engaged, no longer sequestered with other students who just didn't get it. In mixed-achievement-level classes, struggling students learned from the higher-achieving students. With only one course preparation, I had time to think. We got to know the students well. We still had the same number of students, so this was not more costly, but lifting the teaching burden of five classes a day with different courses dramatically changed our work. We would discuss literature, the students would have a break; they returned to class and wrote wonderful essays on their ideas. It was magic. It was real school. For everyone.

Students formed their own study groups out of need. These were the urban students formerly short-changed or dismissed, the "discipline" problems. But newly motivated in our team-based program, many of our students took two city buses across town in the early morning dark to meet in the library before school to process information, to compare homework, to discuss and help each other learn.

Students who predictably would have dropped out of school told me they were going to graduate and go to college to become a history teacher like my teaching partner. John had attended private boarding schools and only knew how to show respect and support for each student. It was how he had been taught. John engaged students in thinking and ideas. Now inspired by school, a student told me she had arranged to spend an extra year in high school so she could attend our state college. One African American student told me she was going "to learn computers to break out of all this." I understood *all this*, the poverty cycle. I marveled at the students. School was serving them.

Sizer's program was a national Coalition of Essential Schools. Our local program was called, improbably, "Hope Essential." A central concept of Sizer's coalition was that all students would learn the same things, in ways appropriate for them. This was radically different. It was also the beginnings of thinking on common state and national standards, to teach and assess the same learning of all students. Sizer was ahead of his time. If we had been handed certain learning standards for all our students to understand, would we have knocked ourselves out to ensure our students mastered them? You bet. Out of personal and professional pride. Also, to make sure our urban students learned national standards.

With this new team program, we saw the change in student attitudes, motivation, and performance. Our students were in a close subgroup that formed its own common expectations: hence learning. We were turning these urban kids—earlier they would have been lost—into students, providing them with the learning that could lead to greater successes. But we had no hard data, no achievement data, not even attendance data, to prove students were learning more.

Again, as administrations changed, so did the school. With Sizer's program working, our program was eliminated. The plan was to create different smaller "houses" in the whole building. The school quickly fell into the lowest school accountability level of "Restructuring" status under the federal No Child Left Behind regulations. Ironically, the program that *wasn't* leaving students behind was eliminated. I hear reports that things now work better. However, nothing comes close to the dramatic successes of turning students around that we had attained earlier. But without hard data, we had nothing to show others that our program worked for students.

For these and other reasons, I salute national learning Standards and tests. Successes are reported and needs revealed and supported. Teachers talk and problem-solve together.

With Common Core national Standards, assessments, and public reporting, classroom achievement is brought to the attention of administrators and the public. The national tests provide us with data on learning of all students. Are test scores a perfect measure? No. But they're what we have to work with. Information is provided on what will be tested. Teachers work to help each student learn these key areas.

Today's test results get to the heart of our work in schools, which is student learning. Easily accessed web-based Standards guide learning from year to year. For this program of common Standards and assessments for all, we thank those at the top—the governors, state school commissioners and administrators, and federal officials. Left to our own devices to make curriculum decisions on what should be taught and when, we'd still be debating this in the schools.

Most of the national Common Core State Standards are what we teach anyway—or should be teaching—in such a way that all students retain the knowledge. The national Standards are fundamentals of reading, writing and math. But teachers need the big picture understandings, support and resources to make this major shift to serve all students well. It doesn't just happen.

The state math tests in many states and in the Common Core Standards ask students to explain a math problem and answer in writing how the problem is solved. Students must show math understanding, not memorization of algorithms. Grade-level mastery Standards build from year to year on the previous year's learning.

On literacy tests, students have to write about a central idea in a passage they're given, answer questions on close reading and inference, and write in different ways for different purposes. Students must learn to use context clues for vocabulary understanding. What was once high-level literary analysis reserved only for some students—how word choice affects point of view and tone, the proficient reading of complex text—is now expected of each student. We can select text close to our students to help them learn these process Standards. The Writing Standards of research and assessing sources in today's information-rich world is required of each student.

I marvel that critics charge these Standards and tests as unfair. Unfair is not having common standards for every child, the privileged and the underprivileged.

These Standards are good guides for teachers and prescribe good skills for students to learn. Many teachers now take pride in seeing their students' scores increase after teaching the specific learning needed and tested. Teachers still have freedom in *how* to teach. Research tells us that students do best on the state tests when the curriculum isn't narrowed to teach only to the test. Most teachers don't just teach for test questions; they integrate the Standards into their teaching. When teachers team up and integrate Standards, their students' test scores soar, verifying learning. Great teachers can still be great teachers. The test scores correlate with teaching effectiveness. Ineffective teachers, or those who ignore the Standards, will be revealed in test score results over time. Is this unfair? No, cheating our students of important learning is unfair.

When teachers can team up, we can boost one another's spirits, help one another through the tough issues, celebrate successes, bring common purpose, and work together to acclimate students to our teaching and learning modes. Preparing students for Standards learning is hard to do alone. It was working with my teammate John that made me a better teacher.

Students whom we might have thought would never be able to work in a certain way on a focused topic can learn to do this well. We can change students. I saw this in our brief bright period of a transformed public school program, which carved out a successful, grand, if short-lived experiment. Teaching common Standards means all students learn better. We needn't cheat the top-achieving students; they still can and must be challenged.

Bright students are limited by standards, critics say. But if some students know the Standards, they can work at a higher level. This is how high-demographic schools function.

The other argument is that Standards restrict teachers' freedom. But teachers have the freedom to be inventive in how they teach. This is explicitly stated in the Standards documents.

Teaching no longer is private practice. We can't afford it. Most compelling is the growing gap between those students who succeed and those who will go unprepared out into a world where low-level jobs are disappearing, replaced by jobs requiring higher technical skills. The rapid technology infusion leaves poorly educated students behind. One must know how to read, write, reason, research, and understand math. Our students' lives depend on this. Getting them there is well worth our hard work.

As a teacher who has seen students transformed, and as a school system administrator who has viewed learning issues from the balcony, I understand why these Standards and tests are good. Without outside test scores based on information that we're provided well in advance, we have no strong measure of our students' learning. Now learning—for all students—is at the heart of school.

The test isn't the end-all and be-all. But it is an indicator of learning. Learning must be the center of the work. Assessments are an important measure of achievement. Qualitative observations are important. But we also must have hard data to see if students really are learning, if teachers are teaching in such a way that students learn and are following a reasonable framework of study, rather than the earlier period of curriculum chaos.

If students do quickly learn and know the Standards understandings, that's wonderful. Teachers are then free to support higher level learning. Common Core Standards are not a limitation but a guarantor of minimal competency.

Developing common Standards learning isn't easy or without stress and anxiety, but teaching never has been easy. Having evidence from outside test scores data is something small in the varied interactions and activity of school. State testing is viewed by many school people as disruptive to a school. State tests to provide outside objective assessments are criticized as taking time away from learning.

But the results are what we can learn from, and what we can show others—parents, administrators, the community, and colleagues—as one piece of evidence that our students have learned. Test results are open to public scrutiny, as they should be.

We have the privilege and responsibility to help all students. We can exult in our successes. Success should be saluted, and needs noted.

With Common Core Standards at each grade level nationally, all students, including the struggling ones, have a fairer shot in life when the same Standards are taught, beginning in the early grades. National Standards bring national resources to help with the Standards learning.

Seeing outside test results on national Standards is a point of pride that shows that, as a teacher, one has served all students well.

Chapter Three

Seeing What Our Students Can Do: One Model

Technology is both annoying and helpful in schools today. Students cleverly defy school rules that smartphones be turned off during the school day. But how else can they communicate with friends and maintain a social life, so essential to young people?

A few years ago I was asked to administer an Advanced Placement test in a high-demographic public high school with lots of relatively privileged, smart, well-mannered kids. These were the "good kids." And they had super-smart, always respectful, devoted teachers. Who wouldn't love to teach these top students in an elite school?

I was serving in this school system as the district Curriculum Director, but I was a former urban school teacher—where we had no AP courses. I had never had to oversee national test-taking. So I asked one of our sharp young English teachers to help me out by reading the testing administration rules and then setting up the test with the students. Once the testing was set up, she could leave and I would sit and pretend I knew what I was doing. She graciously agreed.

This popular, knowledgeable teacher greeted each student warmly, often by name. The students responded nicely in kind, creating a relaxed atmosphere for this high-stakes test with scores that are sent to prospective colleges for college acceptance decisions.

At the time, there was a ban on cell phones in school. Claire welcomed the group and then matter-of-factly said she was passing around a hat they were to put their cell phones in. She explained that she would leave the hat on the front desk and they could pick up their cell phones as they left the testing room. The students politely complied.

Generally, however, we can't keep electronics out of the classroom. A principal tells me that students text while holding their phones under their desktops. They've developed muscle memory for the keys and can text without looking at the phone. And of course they use texting slang or shorthand that drives teachers up the wall when it slips into student writings.

So we have to co-opt student use of technology in the classroom to ensure that the technology is used for learning. One class project I was involved with is a good example of how teachers can let students use technology for learning, even incorporating their social media skills.

When my superintendent asked me to lead a 21st Century Skills Initiative in our district, I formed a committee of parents, students, school committee members, a principal, assistant principal, school technology integration specialist, and our district technology director; the superintendent also attended. My hope was that we could discuss how 21st Century Skills— which include technology—could be introduced and used well.

I had asked a student to report to our committee on his class research project. All our committee members saw that it was an exciting project. I realized that this high-level project unintentionally addressed almost all of the Common Core Reading and Writing Standards.

Everything the student reported on sparked our attention. This is an example of how strong school work can naturally mesh with Standards. Common Core Standards needn't inhibit inventive, interesting projects that engage students and excite them about learning, propelling them to higher levels of learning. In fact, Standards promote creative learning opportunities for students to acquire the needed understandings because we must be inventive for students to learn the more rigorous Standards learning.

Research has yet to show that students learn more with technology use. However, we see anecdotally that students can make huge leaps forward when we take advantage of technology to let them learn important content area skills and understandings.

Some feel that Standards learning and technology use are in two different compartments. But they can be conjoined. When we "flip" teaching and learning to have students engage in research to learn the content and skills of the discipline in substantive ways, they also expand their knowledge with digital literacy. We flip learning when students are working on computers and the teacher guides instead of being at the front of the room talking *at* students and being the sage on the stage while students zone out. Research is one way we can harness technology for learning. Studies show that learning improves with project-based learning; technology is the perfect tool to power project-based learning.

So without fully understanding a project that I vaguely knew was done in our schools, at one of our 21st Century committee sessions I asked Greg to present his National History Day project. Toggling easily back and forth between two web sites he had created for the National History Day competitive project, last year's on the theme of Innovation and the current year's web site reporting his research on the Spanish-American War, Greg focused on the 21st Century Skills he and his peers had used to create their presentations. He didn't intend to be quoting almost directly from a book we were using to create common understanding (Trilling and Fadel's *21st Century Skills: Learning for Life in Our Times*, 2009)—he was simply reporting to us what he did in creating these sites—but he provided a textbook case of learning the book argues for.

In this annual national history project, students must use a web site template to present their research findings. Allowed word counts are limited, forcing students to be succinct and cogent without plagiarizing lengthier text. The students can't ramble. I marveled at how this requirement alone forces careful thought, cutting to the core of the concept and findings being studied. Critics fear that Common Core State Standards inhibit strong learning. Clearly, they do not.

I had helped judge the National History Day school student presentations in an earlier evening session attended by parents and community members attended. I was a judge for a student whose research was on "The Trail of Tears." This project showed the student's research on the 1838 forcible removal under President Andrew Jackson of more than 16,000 Cherokees from their homelands in Tennessee, Alabama, North Carolina, and Georgia. The Native Americans were sent to reservations in what is now Oklahoma. Hundreds of Cherokees died during their trip west, and thousands more perished from the consequences of relocation. The student had extensively researched this period in U.S. history. He simply reported the facts, revealing information, but in his presentation to me he implied a point of view, which is a Common Core Reading Standard understanding. From his research, the student saw that the U.S. government had cruelly pushed people out of their homelands and in many cases to their deaths. The student told me he went to the Boston Public Library for most of his research. I understood that he meant that he had gone on-line for the research; he thus had a vast source of information at his fingertips.

Greg and his team also used primary sources, as did other students in this project. For the Innovation theme, Greg personally interviewed musicians. His research topic was how Les Paul was an innovator of the guitar. Would a tenth grader enjoy that? In their second project the next year, one student on Greg's team located (on-line, of course) all the professors in the Boston area who had a specialty in the team's topic. The team e-mailed each of these professors. Greg reported to us that one professor replied that he "normally he doesn't respond to such outside e-mails, [but] since we had asked such a good question, he would answer." A high school junior receiving that kind of praise from a college professor gains confidence. The need to know and having an open field to research had provided the students with sufficient information and context to develop a strong research question that impressed an expert in the field. And we say that today's students don't use the internet well for learning. Perhaps they can.

Greg's group interviewed this professor via Skype without having to trudge into Boston; they were using worldwide resources from school and home. The team e-mailed each other at night, not always having to have face-to-face meetings since they were already on the same page from their in-school meetings. The team elected to confer at night, when students are on their computers anyway. Pushing homework completion—an onerous task parents know only too well—was replaced with volunteer homework.

Creating Positive Collegial, Collaborative School Culture

Technology can affect school culture when courses connect naturally with other teachers' work while maintaining the integrity of each discipline. Common Core Standards promote common learning across the subject areas, reinforcing the same reading and writing skills in different subjects.

At one meeting the Social Studies department head thanked other departments for letting students work on their research projects during their own classes. The Art Department chair responded, "Well, they were doing graphic arts." So they were. In Greg's project, the team members sought the right political cartoon to convey what they were learning. Common Core Reading Anchor Standard Seven advises, "Integrate and evaluate content presented in diverse media and formats, including visually . . ." The students delighted in finding graphics that reinforced their thinking on the research topic text. The matching of text and graphics was compelling, fun "work," key in Standards learning. Primary sources, graphics, video, and sound were all available to students in their targeted internet research. These young people didn't miss this opportunity to enhance their research presentation, learning new tech skills.

Technology can be the base for disciplines to work together. When the web site template was too constraining for their expanding relevant material, Greg used his programming skills to add information. Were English teachers happy that students were learning the research process? They were thrilled.

Subject area skills need not be boxed into separate courses. When we teach the same skills in different disciplines, as expected with Common Core Standards, students are more apt to learn and retain knowledge. Also, students see how one class's skills connect with another's area, even with real life, not confined to the four walls of just one subject's classroom.

Skills and Understandings for Today and the Future

As Greg casually presented his two research projects to our committee, we all sat stunned but proud. Our district Technology director delightedly remarked, "This is how businesses are started today. People do research and create their own web site." Voila! A business is born.

To say we were impressed by how much the students had learned in this project is an understatement. The teachers were coaches, asking students to refine their question, guiding them. "We were assertive in going to our teacher with questions," Greg stated. Need to know propels learning.

"You'll never forget this project," I told the student who did the "Trail of Tears" research. His enthusiasm was palpable. He continued to talk with me about what he had learned in his in-depth research. The students had learned one topic in history well. But they also acquired and learned to use the skills for researching any other topic. These students also discovered that they could learn on their own. Nothing was too hard for them, especially as a group when tasks were distributed. They learned digital literacy skills that could carry them into any new application, vaulting barriers.

Resilience

Despite their extensive, inventive work, Greg's team didn't win at the state level (others from the school did, and went on to the national competition in Washington, D.C.). Resilience is a 21st Century Skill. We try and we fail. We learn to pivot.

When his sensitive teacher asked the team if they were ready to talk about it, they told her, "Oh, sure. We overheard our judges earlier saying they didn't like all the extra bells and whistles on the web sites." When will more adults learn to value innovation, technology for learning? Technology use for research is expected under Common Core State Standards.

I saw Greg later in the spring and congratulated him for winning at the state Science Fair, held at MIT. "I was surprised," he said. Expect the unexpected. Risk and try again. Carry the skills into a new area.

The school gave Greg an award for his History Day project and his natural voluntary assistance with other students. Greg still mentors other students in their history projects. He's ready for college and the 21st century workplace. Watch out for Greg. He and the other students learned they can learn new areas; he understands how research ability is a powerful tool; he's flexible and adaptable; he learned how to collaborate effectively with others; he learned to go to others for assistance. He gained confidence and competence from his challenging in-depth project. Greg didn't win the competition, but he gained an internal sense of success. He understands that others who judge might have another perspective, but that won't keep him down.

Let's serve all students to help them advance on their own, to see what they're capable of doing. Common Core Standards set this standard. Technology can help immensely.

Standards Learning through Strong Projects

Though it was not conceived to address Common Core national Standards, Greg's research project nonetheless developed 18 of the 20 Common Core Reading and Writing Standards—close reading, inference, central idea, research, argument and expository writing, how point of view shapes content and style, comparing texts and text and visuals, evidence-based argument, critical analysis, and close study of informational text, among others.

Students learn these Standards from doing the work on their own, under their teachers' guidance, and within the constraints of the project guidelines. Students become excited about their learning in part because they can choose the topic of their work. In Greg's case, they discovered, considered, and shaped information on their own. By developing concise thesis statements and web site posts, they distilled information for clarity in thinking.

Common Core State Standards recognize that research ability is essential for our students' future learning and for today's world. A section of the Common Core Writing Standards in three of the ten Standards is devoted to "Research to Build and Present Knowledge." In addition, Standard Six is "Use technology, including the Internet, to produce and publish writing." Common Core Reading Standard Ten is "Read complex text proficiently," which students did on their own from self-initiated learning. No one handed them challenging text and said, "Read this." They self-selected complex text, with ownership of their work. Why do students act out, disrupt a class? Perhaps if we can touch an area of interest for them, they become real students. Common Core State Standards urge us to find this student interest, not work from teacher interest.

Missed Opportunities

With Greg's excellent student project, we have three concerns.

First, it would have been easy for each student to have written up a formal research paper on the topic. The students had spent so much time researching, discussing, learning from one another, making choices on posted items, and debating points. They knew their topic well. A final research paper would have been excellent practice in writing either an argument piece or expository writing, Common Core Writing Standards One and

Two. Writing a research paper—once deadly dull and only expected in "top track" classes—is an important traditional English and social studies course ability. Research papers are common school practice. Writing them is a requirement for college. Knowing these skills is a requirement for the modern workplace. Is it too much to ask that we expect this Common Core Standard of research and writing of every student? Time would have been well spent to develop this ability with each student on Greg's project, and having explored the topic so well, it would have been an easy, fun assignment for them to have transferred their points of view on the topic into the argumentative or essay writing called for by the Common Core Standards. The nonfiction, informational reading that is key in national Standards and is heavily tested on state tests was accomplished well in this project. Students must learn to read and comprehend informational text to continue their learning after leaving high school.

Another concern is that this project was a required assignment only for Honors level students. It was optional for the College Prep level and was not included for the general level.

But students in the "lower level" classes would have been innovative, more engaged in their course work, more excited about this project, and might have performed as well as Honors students. With topic choice, we gain student buy-in, powerful for learning. Too often we withhold more engaging projects from students perceived as "less smart." How do the other students feel, knowing that it's only the Honors students who do this type of research project? Does this enhance their sense of competence and confidence in learning? Even if the results proved not as strong, the other students would have learned from whatever level of accomplishment they reached. And we may be pleasantly surprised with the research work of a student who in the past wasn't deemed capable of self-directed research. With the Common Core expectations of each student learning research, and collaborating on writing, state Standards make learning common, similar in expectations, and even more fun for all. Technology makes this easier. But when we have the goal of only the best and brightest doing the most engaging work, we're simply reinforcing the old achievement gap that Common Core Standards are designed to help us to overcome.

A last concern is that students were advised that if they weren't comfortable with technology they should use a paper tripartite presentation. But in this age of digital literacy, we must develop all students' ability to use technology for learning.

In an information-rich world where sifting through information leads to greater understanding and unleashing the potential of each child, we can't limit the challenging projects to only some of our students.

Chapter Four

How Did We Get Here?

From *A Nation at Risk* to National Common Core State Standards and Race to the Top

> *"The White House has agreed to work with the governors to develop a set of national performance goals, for the first time in history, to guarantee that Americans will have an education system second to none."*
> — Governor Bill Clinton, 1989

Common Core State Standards didn't spring suddenly from the brain of the Obama administration but are a logical next step in a more than 25-year search for national school improvement, essentially moving from separate state standards and tests to national Standards and national tests, for common high-level learning.

The National Commission on Excellence in Education report *A Nation at Risk* (1983) cited a "rising tide of mediocrity" with concern that other countries were outperforming the United States in quality of education. *A Nation at Risk* stimulated discussion of how to improve schools. One response was a 1988 amendment to the 1965 Elementary and Secondary School Improvement Act. The amendment initiated voluntary state-level tests for trial assessments in mathematics and reading. Its language, "Identifying appropriate achievement goals for each age and grade in each subject are to be tested," marked a national cultural shift in schools to create learning goals and to test learning results on the goals. Sanctions were placed on schools and districts that performed poorly.

So the implication of the new Standards isn't new.

A series of governors' conferences in the late 1980s focused discussion on the need for schools to improve. At the 1989 Governors Summit on Education consensus was reached for students in grades 4, 8, and 12 to be tested to assess proficiency. This requirement was presented in President George H. W. Bush's 1990 State of the Union speech.

State curriculum frameworks were published in the early 1990s, and state tests were implemented with the goal of better preparing students and assessing their learning; the frameworks and tests varied from state to state.

The George W. Bush-era No Child Left Behind legislation of 2002, with strong congressional bipartisan support, aimed to move all students to proficient learning on state Standards by 2014, with sanctions if schools fell behind in even one student "subgroup" of traditionally underperforming student groups. The wide disparity of state standards of the 1990s, resulting in very different state-to-state achievement levels to reach "Proficient," logically led to national common Standards. The new Standards came from a study group of content area experts and were based on the goals of organizations such as the National Council of Teachers of English and the National Council of Teachers of Mathematics, leaders in their respective areas.

Anticipating congressional nonrenewal of the No Child Left Behind Act, an impatient Obama administration constructed a new national program, Race to the Top. States were asked to apply to compete for federal approval and accompanying funding to bring this program to their own states; statewide acceptance of program goals and practices was required.

Race to the Top called for not only higher common standards and tests, but also common higher level educator evaluation. A piece of this evaluation includes a teacher's multi-year test scores, intended to push teachers to raise learning levels for all students. Fourteen states promote these more stringent goals.

National Common Core State Standards were published in 2010–11. These new higher level Standards include a new measure of accountability based on student growth rather than attainment of the "Proficient" level. Accountability changed to favoring struggling students over high-demographic districts in looking for annual growth, not requiring the goal of Proficient.

In addition, Race to the Top aims only to narrow the achievement gap, not close it, and no longer counts the same student in as many as five categories—each subgroup and in the aggregate—which punished urban districts.

Thus, since the late 1980s, our country has had over a dozen years of standards and testing programs nationally. States, school systems, and schools require high expectations of all students in the fight to raise the bar as well as to change the pattern of demographics determining destiny.

Many current teachers have taken the state standards tests as students themselves; this isn't new to them. Popularizing research-based best learning practice helps. Along with incremental moves toward higher student achievement at the national policy level, new research and practice to support struggling students have come from the education field and been brought to life in classrooms. These strategies include extended time on learning, one-on-one tutoring, differentiated learning, collaborative student work to learn from peers, project-based learning, and incorporating technology for learning.

Schools and teachers experiment and learn.

This process of education reform with top-down regulations and new methods of teaching has brought incremental change to schools, primarily in the laudable attempts to upgrade standards for all students.

There's no question that teachers are anxious and need support. Understandably, the intent to include all teachers in Standards learning practice is met at times with teacher resentment and resistance. Other teachers pick up the challenge, learn, and take on new practices and work together to solve problems. Can schools and teachers continue to withstand the national and federal pressure for higher performance, especially with traditionally underperforming students? Many try. This is a national experiment.

The goals are laudable. When we see a child fail to learn to read, or encounter a jobless young person in the ever-widening gap between "achievers" and unemployed, we are reminded that common Standards learning is a must. For decades, the education community has tried to help all students learn at higher levels. Now the bar is raised yet again. From the old practice of schools losing too many students to raising the quality of learning for all students, national Standards set the stage for controversy, but also for many in schools to work to meet the challenge. As a nation, do we have the will and understanding to support such a formidable but essential goal: for all students to have equal opportunity to a first-class education?

Sources:
Vinovskis, M (1999). *The Road to Charlottesville: The 1989 Summit*, Paper presented, A Publication of the National Education Goals Panel.

DuFour, R., DuFour, R., Eaker, R (2008). *Revisiting Professional Learning Communities at Work: New Insights for Improving Schools*, Bloomington, IN: Solution Tree Press.

Chapter Five

Developing High-Level Reading Ability

The Big Picture of Reading

We read for information and to make meaning for our lives. We read for pleasure and for new ideas. We love being transported to new worlds through reading and seeing how ideas and people connect with and extend our own understanding. Reading gives us insights into others' lives and our own. We're inspired and motivated from reading. We would be simple, more ignorant—in the sense of not having understanding or being informed—without reading.

Learning to read well is essential to learning. Common Core Standards raise the bar on reading ability expectations. Assessing ability to read grade-level appropriate material with relative proficiency by third grade is not only fair, it's a requirement for a child's life. Learning goes on without the child when he or she lacks third-grade reading ability. Some children may catch up later, but much is lost when one is behind peers.

Reading instruction can't stop at the third grade. Under Common Core Standards, the axiom no longer holds that a goal through third grade is teaching learning to read but by fourth grade children "read to learn." Teaching *how* to read now continues through all the grades and across content areas. The Standards offer good learning guides for each grade level, seeking common grade-level learning.

Common Core State Standards ask that we help students learn *how* to read at higher and higher levels through all grades. These national Standards ask that we don't let some students slip behind. And reading means understanding the complex features and levels of text so that one gains analysis ability.

With Standards guiding teaching, students learn that the author has a point of view. Students learn how word choice shapes meaning or tone. With access to vast, varied readings on the internet, we want to help students learn to be critical thinkers who know how to analyze point of view and purpose. Readers must become sufficiently sophisticated to judge the writer's intent and bias rather than merely taking written information as objective truth. A student may well come across a satirical piece on the internet. He or she must be able to discern purpose. We don't want students accepting opinions without assessing the writer's intent and the connotations, or associations, of the stated words. Standards learning is intentional and aims to ensure analysis and discernment for all.

Standards learning expects schools to develop activities that help all students to read closely for explicit information, inference, central ideas, and word choice for intent; to use context clues for vocabulary development; to evaluate arguments and claims; to compare texts; and to read complex text proficiently.

New Content Expectations in Teaching Reading

How to read is so important that not only English language arts teachers but also science and social studies teachers are now asked to reinforce students' ability to read content area text more carefully.

Students are asked to follow the Common Core reading guides of close reading, inference, main idea, and critical analysis of text, and read complex text. Often sixth-grade teachers of science and social studies despair that many students can't read their content texts. Now these other subject teachers are asked to help shoulder the responsibility of teaching *how* to read and write. This can only help students, but it is also of value to teachers. As Standards learning advances, teachers will find students coming into their grade levels having been taught the same reading skills. In addition, students will advance in content understanding when science and social studies teachers teach the skills of *how* to read their content areas.

Standards grade-level guides bump students up to the next level in reading ability, reinforcing learning over the grade levels and across the disciplines. This prepares students to leave our public schools with the ability to continue to learn on their own and to be informed citizens, analyzing and critiquing text, not simply accepting what a writer—or the media—says as truth. Critical readers can carry these skills to consumption of other media such as film and television. The expert reader sees nuances in film and video that a less informed reader may miss. All students need this ability; it's an essential life skill.

Grade-level Standards learning means that one may have to work individually on focused reading areas with a child and/or in small-group learning with struggling students. Individual reading instruction is the common teaching mode at the elementary level, but with Common Core Standards, content area teachers and upper-grade teachers are also asked to teach individuals. We must ensure that students learn these reading abilities and understandings at each grade level, to help bring all students to reading mastery. Teachers can no longer sail through text that is beyond the reader's ability; they must bring the reader closer to comprehension.

Informational Text

Another key Reading Standards concept is that students read more informational text. The Common Core tenth-grade English test is 75 percent nonfiction text. The intent of this emphasis on informational text is to enable students to continue to learn throughout their lives in our rapidly changing world.

English teachers are needlessly fearful that they will have to set aside beloved literature. But we can add supplementary nonfiction that connects with great literature, such as historical informational readings on such periods as the civil rights movement. Students can read current news articles that connect with ideas of literature and read film reviews for argument analysis. We can stimulate students' love of reading by letting them select biographical subjects from their favorite athletes, film stars, authors, musicians, scientists. And we can expand their horizons by guiding them to books on figures previously unknown to then, an Amelia Earhart or Langston Hughes, a Steve Jobs or an early president.

Foundational Skills

A key area of teaching children how to read is guiding them to an early mastery of phonemic awareness and word decoding, so that they grasp how to understand a word. Some children may come into kindergarten appearing to know how to read. But some are sight readers. Knowing words from having been read to at home is a huge advantage to reading development. However, sight readers hit a wall at third grade, when text becomes more challenging, if they haven't developed the phonics and decoding skills. We have to catch sight readers early on so they learn to sound out new words. Common Core Standards simply reinforce these traditional early reading skills.

When we see that younger children do know phonics and have early reading ability, we provide them with "leveled" texts at or above their independent reading level. Student interest plays a big role. We know that students can read more complex text when they're intrigued by the topic. This develops their reading ability, helping to support the growth of all readers. It's not uncommon for teachers to purchase their own books for particular students or a particular class. We feel it's worth our money. Common Core Standard Ten is "Read complex text proficiently," always helping students move to the next best step in reading. "Baby steps" is a technical learning term. "Just right" reading is also a technical term, in which students read at their independent level. The term "Instructional level" for elementary reading is one at which children are taught in the classroom. Common Core Standards simply remind us of this good practice.

Many elementary schools use a reading technique in which books are strictly leveled by text complexity and students are grouped by where they are in reading development. This is an excellent approach, as long as each group is well served. But sometimes a struggling reader is assigned to a teacher's aide, who may or may not be qualified to help this student advance in reading development. The more qualified teacher should be the one who helps this child. In addition, direct instruction or other learning methods may be needed to suit a child's learning style. This Common Core Standards area of early reading development is just traditional best practice. A fine point debated with Standard Ten is that children should not be pushed too far beyond text the child can read. Informed, sensitive elementary teachers—who are the vast majority—maintain the balance that's right for the child.

Helping Special Education Students Learn to Read

Special education teachers often feel their students are underserved in "flexible grouping" teaching methods, when they know that their students may require one-on-one direct instruction that meets the child's reading needs. "Inclusion" can be a disservice to special needs students if their needs are not being met. In reviewing early grade-level state test scores, a team of special education team chairs found that students who had been provided the individualized direct reading instruction of skilled reading specialists performed better than students who were in inclusion classes. When special needs students with a disability that interferes with learning are provided one-on-one instruction in their area of needs, as well as the classroom inclusion learning, students often break the code and learn to read.

Teachers are at times impossibly stretched in a classroom. A teacher can't always provide the individualized attention struggling students need in a large class. But inclusion means all students are included in the learning, not just sitting in the classroom. At the upper-grade levels, regular education teachers often have classes with many special education students. While the teachers in one high school were proud of the fact that every student read the same texts, many struggling readers were lost with text that was far above their reading ability. This was loss of precious learning time for these needy students. The financial costs of providing specialized reading instruction to needy students is far outweighed by learning success. What is more important than unlocking the doorway to reading for nonreaders, or helping students comprehend at a higher level? Common Core supports common learning.

One reading specialist was told by her daughter's school that her special needs child would never learn to read. Knowing well the early foundational skills, this teacher-parent worked on her own with her daughter on phonics, rhyming words, word recognition, and moving on to comprehension. Her daughter is now a reader.

Another special education teacher who was told her child wouldn't be able to read determinedly arranged to have one-on-one direct instruction three times a week with a special education Wilson reading program. With careful instruction, her daughter broke the code of reading. Small miracles that change a child's life can happen. We need more of these examples of individualized intervention. Again, Common Core urges this key learning for future success, a guide for all schools to follow as best they can.

A Book for Every Child

Fortunately, we're lucky in the English language arts area to have a multitude of readings to suit each child. There are high-interest, easy-reading books for all grade levels to support struggling readers. Differentiating learning in the ELA area is doable. We needn't teach in one-size-fits-all land.

Engaging Readers in Text Ideas—the "Hook"

Even when we may not have materials that can match students' needs and interests, the particular angle we take can engage students. Teaching the challenging *The Scarlet Letter* can engage students when they are outraged at the persecution of Hester Prynne while the weak males hide their culpability. We can't always predict what book will engage a class, or a child, and we love it when a book does capture interest. This is the perfect teachable moment for higher-level learning. By taking an idea that captures students, teachers can guide them to read and explore the ideas of complex text. A text students may not be able to read on their own becomes accessible with guided discussions and an idea that fascinates them.

Teacher Style and Flexibility

One third-grade teacher with an excellent background in reading development always purchased her own books. She taught with her own teaching style, which was energetic, informed, knowledgeable, and dedicated to each child. She was a dynamic, expert teacher of reading. Her principal was a devoted reading expert herself and permitted this teacher to teach as she wished and not follow the school's program. This principal—a lover of reading—saw the classes and also the results. Importantly, this teacher's success in reading instruction was confirmed with objective outside test scores consistently above all others in the school, and the school's English language arts state test scores always ranked higher than the other elementary schools in the district. Common Core State Standards needn't inhibit individual style, especially when results are impressive.

However, another teacher was a graduate of an arts college. With a Master of Arts degree in literacy, she had learned only one philosophy and practice. "I only know how to teach reading in this one way," she commented. But this teacher understood collaboration. State test scores showed that the school was not teaching students to read for explicitly stated information. The school reading specialist recommended purchase of a supplemental program of direct instruction on reading skills. This teacher learned how to supplement her reading instruction with direct instruction material. National Standards ask us to be flexible to address student needs. The issue raised with Common Core Standards is, are the students learning?

Tailoring Instruction to the Student

The expert reading specialist at one school always apologized that when I visited the school I saw that she was pulling students out of classes to work individually with them on their reading development. This reading specialist had a range of books and materials in her room and was adept at matching learning with needs. She was a highly skilled professional. I kept telling her not to apologize. While "pullout" has been disparaged, it *can* be the best practice when a specialist has the expertise to target growth.

Co-Teaching

Our move toward "inclusion" needs to be with the caution that when struggling students are included in a regular classroom they should still be provided appropriate learning support. We wonder why special needs students can be "discipline problems" when in the regular classroom. A good strategy is co-teaching, when a regular education English language arts teacher co-teaches with a special education teacher in smaller classes. While this is costly for a school, can we afford not to fund strong learning for struggling students?

School-day planning time for co-teaching is often considered the hurdle. When I co-taught classes with a content teacher, time for planning was not an issue. We met as needed and as possible. We created our own planning time. We had a running conversation through wanting to compare and exchange thoughts. Planning—ensured by teaching adjacent to each other—went smoothly. Teachers who work well together and can learn together and discuss well can overcome the limits of school-allocated meeting time. One department head scheduled regular lunch meetings with one group of teachers with whom he was otherwise unable to meet. Ideally planning time is built into a school schedule. But teachers learn—even expect—to overcome hurdles. We can find the time when we must. Ideally, schools provide teachers time to talk, to take on this challenge of high expectations for each child.

Summing Up Common Core Reading Standards

I roll my eyes when I hear that Common Core Standards "dumb down" learning. When I discuss Standards learning with teachers, their eyes widen. They know that reaching Common Core State Standards for each student is a stretch. But teachers try to make the reach, for themselves as caring professionals and for their students.

Standards learning certainly presents problems, such as finding that unique way to engage a student. For higher-achieving students, we accelerate learning. "Dumbing down" isn't the problem.

Developing students' ability to read is probably the single most important skill for learning growth and, in many cases, survival. Research tells us third-grade reading ability correlates with high school dropout rates. Frustrated with school and falling behind, some students simply depart, leaving a blank where one's future should be. Some quickly pick up reading skills, especially with strong home support, such as being read to by adults. Others learn only gradually. When the gap between adept readers and struggling readers or nonreaders grows, learning development slows. By middle school, a student knows when he or she has been left behind. These are the students who often become challenging, acting out their frustration with school. In high school, a struggling student may well leave school or be expelled as a disciplinary case.

Teaching the skills of reading—at increasingly higher, more complex levels—throughout a student's education is an underpinning of the Common Core Reading Standards.

In the past, and to some degree currently, children who attained reading proficiency with grade-level text and above became the better students who easily accessed text. Reading skills—learning how to read text—have not always been systematically taught at fourth grade and higher. For some children, cracks widen between their own reading ability and that of their peers. Learning then becomes hit or miss when students can't access text.

If students haven't learned to read proficiently by the fifth grade, learning goes on without them in middle school. Remedial help doesn't match the regular classroom work. Students fall further and further behind. The gap widens between what the student is able to do and what is expected in classes. By high school, students are leveled into different courses. Less is expected of those in the "general" level; top-level courses promote high-level learning. The achievement gap between traditionally lower-performing students and higher-achieving students widens. State tests document this. Common Core Standards aim to break this pattern.

In this sense, and others, Common Core grade-level Reading Standards are our savior.

Chapter Six

THE READING STANDARDS

AN OVERVIEW AND PART I: KEY IDEAS AND DETAILS

The Common Core State Standards on Reading constitute simply the main reading and literary analysis standards that traditionally have been taught primarily to higher-achieving students. (*Please see the Reading Anchor Standards below.*)

Common Core asks that we help all students learn the reading skills of close reading, text-based evidence, apt inference, central idea, movement over text, context clues for word meaning, comparing texts and visuals, figurative language of images, how writer's point of view and purpose shapes content and style, and argument evaluation. This is the stuff of reading and critical analysis. These skills and understandings also carry over to analysis of real world problems, asking what are the facts and evidence and how do pieces fit together. The skillful reader learns to read and assess life situations. One learns to question rumor, consider the source of information reporting, understand purpose and goals, see how point of view affects content. These skills help one become an intelligent citizen who betters her own life through facts and analysis and positively affects the lives of others.

The Reading Standards fall specifically into three categories:

• Key Ideas and Details involves close reading of text and inference, main idea, and movement of character, plot, and ideas.

• Craft and Structure pays attention to text word choice, text structure, and point of view or author's purpose.

• Integration of Knowledge and Ideas looks at broader text analysis, not the fine close reading of earlier Standards.

With Craft and Structure, the reader is analyzing text for how message is conveyed and thereby is measuring the quality of writing and is aware of purpose. When text is simple, lacks imagery that conveys meaning, and presents a questionable message, the skillful reader sees lower-quality, even polemical writing. In well-crafted, idea-enhancing text, the reader sees nuance, interesting characters and action, and specific language that conveys meaning.

The Craft and Structure Standards ask that readers learn to assess how point of view or purpose shapes content and style. A clear example is when J. D. Salinger has his protagonist Holden Caulfield, in the classic *The Catcher in the Rye,* cite examples of the "phoniness" he abhors in others. Holden tears characters to shreds but adores those who are caring people, such as his beloved sister Phoebe. Here Salinger conveys his own somewhat cynical view of the world and of others. Holden's younger brother Allie died of leukemia three years earlier; Holden still worships Allie's goodness. This devotion to Allie reinforces Holden's sensitivity and shows the goodness of this otherwise hypercritical young man. Adolescents are drawn to this young man's point of view as they become more worldly themselves, sometimes even critical of their elders.

With the Craft and Structure Standard of author's purpose, the reader views the world through Holden's world, learning to understand the writer's purpose of presenting a world view. With humor and exaggeration, Salinger creates a compelling plea for people to be open, honest, and good to others.

Distinguishing the writer from a first-person narrator is an advanced reading skill, not taught to younger children, one barely grasped developmentally even in later school years. Seeing that an author uses a narrator for the author's purpose broadens thinking. Common Core Standards ask readers to understand and question purpose, a high-level analysis skill. A life skill.

With the third category of Reading Standards, we compare film and text, long a teaching practice to look more closely at similarities and differences to delve into critical analysis of media, as well as informational and fiction reading. A key Knowledge and Ideas Standard is that of argument. Readers are asked to evaluate argument and claims, including validity of reasoning and relevance and sufficiency of evidence. Because we've had a warm spell in New England in January, does this substantiate a counter-argument to scientists' claim of global warming?

Reading Standard Ten asks that students learn to read and comprehend complex text proficiently. When implemented in classrooms, this Standard ensures that children gradually learn to read material of relatively more-challenging vocabulary, more-complex sentences, and more-complex ideas.

Elementary classrooms may move from a simple fable to *Charlotte's Web* to the wonderful Gary Paulsen novels. Middle school students might move to the popular and complex but engaging Harry Potter epic fantasy novels. And high school students progress to traditional classics such as *The Scarlet Letter*; Hawthorne's novel, with its difficult vocabulary, complex sentences and paragraphs, characters who are villains, and a timeless message on harassment, is a strong test of reading ability.

This is the traditional book-reading trajectory over the grade levels. But only the higher-achieving students read and study *The Scarlet Letter*. Common Core asks not necessarily that we punish less able readers with an incomprehensible, possibly remote text, but that we must move all students to increasingly higher-level, more-complex reading.

One high-demographic high school was proud that all of its students read the remote classic *Beowulf*. We thank Hollywood for bringing out the film version, to make sense of otherwise dense, arcane text, but perhaps Stephen Crane's *The Red Badge of Courage* could be a challenging substitute, with more meaning for a generation that has seen war.

The key with the goal of comprehending complex text proficiently is that this is an individual, specially interpreted goal for each student. What is complex for one is an easy read for another, often due to personal interest and background knowledge. Boys are not naturally drawn to the work of Virginia Woolf or Amy Tang. Only the most skillful teacher is successful with this challenge, but young men will avidly read complex, suspenseful science fiction texts.

This deceptively simple final Standard of "Read complex text proficiently" requires that we assess each child's level of reading ability and move each child along with the ability to understand increasingly more and more complex text. This is not an easy task with an elementary classroom of 25 children all at different reading levels, and less so with a middle school teacher's not uncommon load of 120 students a day.

Common Core Standards have high expectations that can be attained, not overnight but over time, and that need strong support for schools to realize these goals, not an easy win.

COMMON CORE ANCHOR STANDARDS FOR READING

Key Ideas and Details

1. Read closely to determine what the text says explicitly and to make logical inferences from it; cite specific textual evidence when writing or speaking to support conclusions drawn from the text.

2. Determine central ideas or themes of a text and analyze their development; summarize the key supporting details and ideas.

3. Analyze how and why individuals, events, and ideas develop and interact over the course of a text.

Craft and Structure

4. Interpret words and phrases as they are used in a text, including determining technical, connotative, and figurative meanings, and analyze how specific word choices shape meaning or tone.

5. Analyze the structure of texts, including how specific sentences, paragraphs, and larger portions of the text (e.g., a section, chapter, scene, or stanza) relate to each other and the whole.

6. Assess how point of view or purpose shapes the content and style of a text.

Integration of Knowledge and Ideas

7. Integrate and evaluate content presented in diverse media and formats, including visually and quantitatively, as well as in words.

8. Delineate and evaluate the argument and specific claims in a text, including the validity of the reasoning as well as the relevance and sufficiency of the evidence.

9. Analyze how two or more texts address similar themes or topics in order to build knowledge or to compare the approaches the authors take.

Range of Reading and Level of Text Complexity

10. Read and comprehend complex literary and informational texts independently and proficiently.

Chapter Seven

The Reading Standards
Part II: Craft and Structure

The Common Core Reading Standards of understanding writers' Craft and Structure include interpreting word meaning from context, how structure pieces connect, and how point of view or purpose shapes content and style.

When we read a sports page article on our beloved home team's tragic loss or exhilarating surprise win, we see the powerful words of condemnation of our hapless athletes or praise as an Olympic god. Next week's loss is a whole different ball game. Now the sports writer damns last week's hero—he's old, he's lost his touch, he's blind, he's incapable of leading. No player or coach is spared, especially not last week's hero. The writer is as joyous as he is ferocious, all depending on the game's outcome. The reader delights in and empathizes with the sports writer's feelings of loss or exultation.

Point of view, writer's purpose, word meaning, word associations and connotation, parts of text connecting with the whole—none are not subtle on the sports page. For many students, Standards learning comes alive using such clear examples.

A newspaper editorial or letter to the editor presents a strong case on an issue with perhaps less verbal freedom in word choice but still with potent force and careful selection of detail.

A science text is factual, informational text. A history piece may provide detail that conveys point of view on a topic. Time changes perspective. The presentation of facts from the 1960s civil rights period now is described with the point of view as a courageous process of gaining human rights. History rewrites itself, an intriguing perspective a student gains in research on a topic.

When a student freely reads pieces on the internet, he or she must be able to assess the source, understand the point of view, balance the piece with other readings, and discern fact from fiction.

Fiction, too, presents a truth. In Shirley Jackson's classic short story "The Lottery," the story simply describes a town that annually holds a lottery. The person who "wins" the lottery is then stoned to death by the townspeople. This is because it's tradition. The lottery is what has always been done in the town. The reader clearly sees the brutality of what is described. The reader understands the author's purpose. The reader understands through detail that the writer's point of view on the topic is that just because something has always been done one way doesn't mean it's right. No townsperson dares to fight the tradition. Can students see themselves and peers as a possible bully—one cruel to others—in this reading?

A strong example of Standard Four, how word choice shapes meaning or tone, is in the classic E. E. Cummings poem "In Just-Spring." This poem celebrates "when the world is mud-luscious" and "puddle-wonderful."

Point of view or purpose is also clear in the content and style of newspaper opinion writing. When the Idaho state legislature passed a law allowing guns on state university campuses, a biology professor published a *New York Times* op-ed piece, "When Can I Shoot My Students?" (Greg Hampikian, February 28, 2014, p. A21). Professor Hampikian argues for proactive self-defense. "Since many of my students are likely to be armed, I thought it would be a good idea to even the playing field . . . I assume that if a student shoots first, I am allowed to empty my clip." Without the skills and understanding of reading for the author's purpose by analysis of content and style, the reader is in danger of taking this satirical piece seriously.

The Craft and Structure Common Core Standards promote all students learning to see how parts fit the whole, how specific word choices shape meaning or tone (Standard Four), how pieces of text relate to each other and the whole (Standard Five), and how point of view or purpose shape the content and style of text (Standard Six). These are Standards that students can easily grasp with the right reading close to the student. Then this analysis is gradually transferred to more complex text. With Standards, the learning of such reading analysis brings insight and critical thinking; critical close reading begins in the early years of school and builds each year to higher levels, slowly building to more sophisticated understanding, with all students. Without Common Core Standards, this type of analysis which more fully informs reading ability is reserved for higher-achieving students. Standards learning invites this learning opportunity for each student.

Vocabulary Development for Greater Reading Comprehension, Expanding Knowledge

Standard Six of Craft and Purpose on "interpret words as they're used in text" builds sensitivity to word meaning in context. Common Core Standards emphasize vocabulary development, especially through context clues to understand word meaning. When in the classic poem "Casey at the Bat," the "Mudville" baseball team is doing poorly, a "pall-like silence fell upon the patrons of the game." The word "patron" is easily learned as those attending the game, a supporter. The careful reader also understands through context that "pall-like" is sad, creating an effect of gloom, associated even with death. The mood is funereal in this first stanza. Connotation in this sense sees "Mudville" as stuck in the mud, a mundane, sad setting. Even their baseball team is a loser. Not all vocabulary can be understood through context clues. Technical terms can be easily defined through the ever-present manual technology devices. A student can go to one's pocket, "Google" a word with a smartphone, and find the definition.

Voracious or at least frequent reading builds vocabulary when the same words are found regularly in context. Reading itself builds vocabulary. When the teacher is teaching how to use context clues to determine word meaning, as Standards urge, the child develops more-nuanced vocabulary that widens understanding and brings new insight.

Author's Point of View or Purpose

Certainly we want all students to broaden their world with understanding of how point of view or purpose shapes content and style: a news report is ideally formal, factual, opinion-free; a poem conveys joy and beauty; a sports article celebrates victory. Students must interpret words and phrases as they're used in the text—"mud" is fun, as in Cummings's poem "In Just-Spring," or sluggish as seen in "Mudville."

Learning writer's craft is interesting and fun—and necessary to a high-quality education.

Chapter Eight

THE READING STANDARDS III: KNOWLEDGE AND IDEAS

The third category of Reading Standards is Integration of Knowledge and Ideas, focusing on a more holistic understanding of text.

COMPARE FILM AND BOOK FOR WHAT IS SAID AND HOW
We love to compare a film with the book on which it is based. We're surprised, possibly annoyed, when the film strays from the book. Or we appreciate a film, then read the book. The book may be exactly the same or have layers of meaning or insight the film lacks. Character portrayal, motivation, and central idea is avidly dissected in film-versus-book analysis, generating heated discussion.

Standard Seven of Knowledge and Ideas is "Integrate and evaluate content presented in diverse media and formats, including visually and quantitatively, as well as in words."

We live in a visual world of film and television. Common Core State Standards recognizes that students are drawn to film, video, TV. The Standards recognize that we must take advantage of students' highly developed sense of visual analysis. Standards bring that learned analysis of media to reading text. The visual is a pathway to understanding text. Students note character detail, setting, plot detail, nuance in film. Standards recognize this and give teachers permission to use the visual as a doorway to literary analysis, critical reading, understanding fine points and layers of meaning in text.

Teachers are thrilled when a traditionally taught book becomes a film, from *Charlotte's Web* to Louis Sachar's middle school book and film, *Holes*, to *Beowulf*, and through the many films of Shakespearean classics that bring remote language alive in character and action, adding meaning. Viewing the film version helps struggling students understand text. Higher-achieving students view the film critically; we delve back into the book for comparison.

Young people develop the reading skill of "prediction" when viewing film. Trained in common plot development, they expect that in film the "good guy" will win in the end. A common twist in film is the underdog outperforming the former top dog who initially underestimates him or her. Students expect to see this in film. In literature, the end note can be a surprise. A film director doesn't dare change the ending of *Romeo and Juliet*. Comparing film and text, or one reading with another reading, is stimulating, creative, and thought-provoking, a common teaching strategy used in classrooms for decades that Common Core Standards recognize and promote. Teachers are thrilled when their students say the book is better. The text-film comparison isn't new to classrooms. But this teaching, formerly scorned, is now sanctified with state Standards, to engage all students.

Compare Texts

Standard Nine is "Analyze how two or more texts address similar themes or topics in order to build knowledge or to compare approaches the authors take."

Teachers know well "compare and contrast," and they commonly use the Venn diagram of intersecting circles at the elementary grades as a graphic to support what is common to two texts and what is different. This comparison of texts and text and visual deepens understanding of each, provokes students to delve more fully into each text and to study each text more closely. These Standards help students build knowledge. The Standards stimulate thinking and critical reading. The more-accessible visual media are a tool that helps us help struggling readers become better readers and invites higher-achieving students to note more carefully similarities and differences. Film-text comparison is an open field for different viewpoints, based on text evidence. The teacher knows not to intervene in good class discussion comparing texts, because the teacher knows the value of developing student thought. The teacher simply monitors discussion. We've done this for decades in school.

Evaluate Argument and Claims for Valid Reasoning and Sufficient Evidence

Reading Standard Eight is "Delineate and evaluate the argument and specific claims in a text, including the validity of reasoning as well as the relevance and sufficiency of the evidence." This Standard recognizes that much of text is presenting a case for a point.

Middle-class white students gain greater understanding of other cultures when they read African American or Latino literature and biography which present the lives of those of another culture. The Standards promote multicultural literature. Specific claims in text can sensitize students to other cultures. Literature that takes a reader into unfamiliar cultures develops empathy. On the other hand, my students from the Dominican Republic shunned a classic African American text but devoured *How the Garcia Girls Lost their Accent* by Julia Alvarez. Though the story was by a middle-class young woman, even the boys in the class loved the connection to their homeland and easily accessed close reading and analysis, resulting in stimulating discussion and excellent writing. They explicated text and levels of analysis to me, their teacher. In this case, nonreaders and writers became readers through a text close to their own life experience that was mostly ignored in school. They delighted in delineation of culture.

Specific claims in a text can be less than subtle. The books of writer Ayn Rand promote individualism over the collective good. Rand is hotly contested. Her books are compelling reading about individual strength. But she refers to egoism as the "virtue of selfishness." My first angry parent conference in one district was with a parent who objected strongly to one teacher's students reading Rand's brief parable *Anthem* (1938). While this simple story can be read from varied viewpoints, some readings and some authors touch a raw nerve. The school and teacher must decide if an argument is acceptable to take on. Banning texts doesn't solve the problem. It only limits students' ability to evaluate argument, a high-level needed skill.

When students learn the critical reading perspective of evaluating argument, evidence and validity, they don't accept surface claims. Teachers most often show good judgment when assessing use of material and how to present it for their particular students.

Teachers often use local newspaper editorials, op-ed pieces, and letters to the editor to evaluate argument, analyze for sufficient and valid evidence, and assess polemical as opposed to evidence-based argument. These readings close to the students allow teachers to use varied levels of text difficulty. The range of readings to assess argument is easily accessed on-line, as well as with varied texts to help develop the same learning with all students. Readings can be accessed from home computers for homework that's compelling, as young people enjoy critical reading and will argue a case via e-mail with peers or in blogging and on-line discussion boards.

Harvard professor Lawrence Kohlberg (1970s) found in his research that in discussions students always ended on the highest level of moral insight. Experience shows that we can most often trust students to reach moral principles in assessing argument. Close reading of evidence and assessing validity of argument is often well-used in school debate. Assessing argument raises all students' ability not to accept superficial stances on an issue.

STANDARD TEN: READ COMPLEX TEXT PROFICIENTLY

Reading Standard Ten simply asks that teachers move each student as appropriate to text that is more and more complex with relatively more-challenging vocabulary, complex sentences and paragraphs, and complexity in thought. While John Steinbeck's novels are often simple in language and sentencing, his work is read most often at the high school level due to the level of analysis. Conversely, Harper Lee's classic, wonderful novel, *To Kill A Mockingbird*, with challenging vocabulary and complex, varied characters and plot, is heatedly debated for middle school readers, while high school teachers also want to teach this warm, heartfelt book of courage told from a child's point of view.

Personal interest trumps text complexity. Students will read complex fantasy and science fiction works when intrigued. My urban students read sports articles at the level of close text reading and critical analysis, while traditional text was indecipherable for them. Young children with a love of animals will read more-challenging text easily. We must capitalize on this personal interest and background context to have students read more complex text and understand it well, then move to somewhat more remote reading, having developed their reading skills in their area of interest.

We can see from this close look at Reading Standards that Common Core State Standards are laudable, ambitious, doable, and necessary.

All students have a richer education with good Standards guidance.

Experimenting for New Learning

I once had what I felt was an inspired idea to take two of my very bright but turned-off-from-school young men to read "guy books," individualized for them.

I gave one a purchased copy of Tobias Wolf's popular autobiographical story of growing up with his family, *This Boy's Life*. To the other, I gave a library copy—risking loss, I knew—of Tobias's brother Geoffrey Wolf's *Duke of Deception*, now sadly out of print. The latter is a hilarious account of his father's magnificent salesmanship, such as talking a car salesman into selling him a car that he never paid for. When that car was repossessed or died, Geoffrey's father (in his telling) simply similarly acquired another one. He never actually paid for a car.

Each book was each brother's account of growing up with the same parents, but they were very different stories with very different experiences and viewpoints.

This reading worked. Each student avidly read his own book, loved it, and wrote well on it.

I had the idea of the two students switching books then discussing the two books together. When I told them this, they just looked at each other. That wasn't going to happen. Sometimes innovative thinking works; experiments fail. We learn to accept mini-successes. Teachers learn and move on.

Chapter Nine

COMMON CORE WRITING STANDARDS

The Common Core State Standards in Writing ask that students are able to write in varied ways for varied purposes and audiences; produce clear and coherent writing with appropriate idea development, organization and style; and become adept at research using print and internet sources. *(See Writing Anchor Standards below.)*

Writing Standards move away from the formulaic writing expected under earlier state Standards. With standards and tests having a powerful effect on classroom instruction, students often learned only to use a contrived formula for writing. This formula was often simply introduction, examples, conclusion.

Common Core Standards release student writers from this confined, confining formula model to develop ideas in writing. Standard Ten urges a range of types of writing, which expands thinking and learning by avoiding a strict pattern of writing on thoughts. Writing generates thoughts. Once thoughts are expressed in writing, then students create the organization that presents thoughts well to the reader, reversing the confining formula previously set through state tests. Certainly for struggling writers a graphic is helpful to set out ideas. Formulaic writing squelches ideas for higher-achieving students; Common Core Standards accelerate writing ability for all students.

Common Core Writing Standards draw schools back to the earlier period of developing the writing process by initially brainstorming, drafting and getting ideas on paper, then having a reader such as a peer check the writing to assist the writer in clarity and idea development, then organization and revision, and final editing. This writing process called "process writing" reverses the set pattern of writing that students learned from earlier state tests. Instead of writing for a form, with Common Core one develops ideas and then moves the writing into organization, and editing, the final step.

We're grateful for this major change in developing strong effective writing that Common Core Standards bring, which helps students more fully develop their writing ability, needed for expression for college, career, and life. One doesn't write in texting format to one's boss; e-mail writing in the world of work must be more formal, aware of audience and purpose.

Instead of one composition pattern assumed as required for writing in the former state tests, Common Core Standards call for varied writing for varied purposes and audiences and also the understanding and skills of three main types of writing. Strikingly, Writing Standard One is Argument writing. Students must be able to present a case for a viewpoint. Evidence-based argument and addressing counterclaims allows one to make one's own case. We don't learn from only one opinion. We learn from hearing a range of viewpoints.

Argument, called Opinion writing at the elementary level, spells out specific facets needed at each grade level, leading to a complex Argument-writing piece by grade 10. The five complex facets required by grade 10 could rarely if ever be accomplished well with students without the prior grade-level stages. We want all students to be clear, in-depth thinkers who can argue a case cogently with evidence.

The second major writing model is the traditional essay, Explanatory writing. This fine Standard sets out annual grade-level facets of expository writing. The second-grade Writing Standard is "Write informative/explanatory texts in which students introduce a topic, use facts and definitions to develop points, and provide a concluding statement or section." Is this "dumbing down" students? We build expository writing from there.

The third Writing Standard is Narrative writing, which includes creative and "how to" writing, such as science writing of how to do an experiment. Creative writing was squelched under earlier state standards, and now with Narrative writing, which includes writing a story, students are free to be inventive and use more colorful, imagistic expression, which carries over into other writing types to improve the quality. This Narrative Writing Standard permits children to develop creative expression, suppressed and even forbidden with earlier standards and tests. After the state testing was completed in schools, creative writing flourished in classrooms and is now expected.

These three main types of writing with specific criteria counter the confining reign of the "five-paragraph essay" of earlier years, which returned under state tests in the 1990s. The process of idea development in writing was promoted nationally through the National Writing Project starting in the 1970s and still exists. With Standards tests, any type of longer composition—Narrative, Argument, or Essay—can be expected at any grade level, ensuring that varied writing types are taught.

Research Standards

Writing Standards Seven through Nine call for use of research to inform writing, a requirement for our ever-changing world with the rapid expansion of technology that generates new knowledge. Students must learn to keep current with events, be able to quickly locate information, validate information from multiple sources, analyze and synthesize information, and present in cogent writing, clearly conveying what one has learned. Not only higher-achieving students must excel with developing research ability and presenting findings coherently, but all students must learn these skills and understandings.

Standards require that documenting sources, always a bane of teachers' life, must be mastered by sixth grade. A student can easily electronically cut and paste others' writing into their own text. YouTube instructional video clips teach students why not and how not to plagiarize text. Electronic applications are the teacher's best friends when they reveal plagiarized text. Technology has its advantages as well as downside for schools today.

Standard Ten: Range of Writing

Writing Standard Ten is Range of Writing. This Standard asks that students "Write routinely over extended time frames (time for research, reflection, and revision) and shorter time frames (a single sitting or a day or two) for a range of tasks, purposes, and audiences."

Frequent Writing With Timely Feedback Promotes Learning

One of the findings of the "90/90/90" study of researcher Doug Reeves showed that in a large scale look at schools with populations of 90 percent minority, 90 percent low income, and 90 percent Proficient is that frequent writing with timely feedback results in student learning improvements in all content areas. The value of frequent writing makes sense. Writing stimulates ideas, forces us to think and process information, and requires us to communicate our ideas effectively to others.

We can thank Common Core State Standards for setting out the goal of frequent writing for varied purposes as opposed to earlier tests that promoted writing in a strict formula. Writing develops one's thinking, allows one to capture ideas, helps explain to others, expands on points, provides evidence to make a case, promotes research with the vast internet resources to capture knowledge and then to present knowledge, breaking free of simple steps that constrain thinking. With Common Core, we learn to write well and write to learn.

Reference
Reeves, Douglas B. (2000). *High Performance in High Poverty Schools: 90/90/90 and Beyond: Accountability in Action*, Read and Learn Publisher.

Common Core Anchor Standards for Writing

Text Types and Purposes

1. Write arguments to support claims in an analysis of substantive topics or texts, using valid reasoning and relevant and sufficient evidence.

2. Write informative/ explanatory texts to examine and convey complex ideas and information clearly and accurately through the effective selection, organization, and analysis of content.

3. Write narratives to develop real or imagined experiences or events using effective technique, well-chosen details, and well-structured event sequences.

Production and Distribution of Writing

4. Produce clear and coherent writing in which the development, organization, and style are appropriate to task, purpose, and audience.

5. Develop and strengthen writing as needed by planning, revising, editing, rewriting, or trying a new approach.

6. Use technology, including the Internet, to produce and publish writing and to interact and collaborate with others.

Research to Build and Present Knowledge

7. Conduct short as well as more sustained research projects based on focused questions, demonstrating understanding of the subject under investigation.

8. Gather relevant information from multiple print and digital sources, assess the credibility and accuracy of each source, and integrate the information while avoiding plagiarism.

9. Draw evidence from literary or informational texts to support analysis, reflection, and research.

Range of Writing

10. Write routinely over extended time frames (time for research, reflection, and revision) and shorter time frames (a single sitting or a day or two) for a range of tasks, purposes, and audiences.

Chapter Ten

A Sea Change

For schools and classrooms that have adhered to the expectations and requirements of national, federal, and state learning standards and testing, this next step up to more-challenging Common Core Standards is hard but not impossible. For states that have had relatively easier standards and tests, it can be a huge leap. The will and skill to make this new stage happen may be lacking in public opinion; parents may feel their hopes for their children are dashed and that teachers are constricted in their teaching. Public understanding and support of Standards learning is welcomed.

Common Core Standards are high level. Acceleration of learning for every child challenges the capability of school, district, and state education leaders who have kept more modest learning expectations. Common Core may seem like a tsunami to classroom teachers who have long worked under an older system that had a sink or swim initiation to teaching—leaving teachers on their own in figuring out what to teach and how. Teachers are now expected to teach more-challenging skills and understandings, to all students, and especially to traditionally underperforming students. It's a triple whammy. Teachers who felt successful because their higher-achieving students learned well can lose their sense of self-confidence when struggling students challenge their ability to teach. Some fight the changes, often stridently, some passively resist, thinking with the many changes that happen in education, "This too will pass." Some leave the profession.

Other practitioners seek knowledge of Common Core Standards learning and try their best to help. Ideally, colleagues work together to understand Standards and share ideas on how to help students gain the needed skills and learning. They work to reach all students. Some school systems provide good professional development which helps teachers better understand and figure out how to apply Standards learning to classrooms. Some teachers are the avant-garde who pick up the banner of "no child left behind" and challenging Standards and even charge ahead despite of or because of school culture. These are the silent saints who by nature or happenstance follow the rules or sense of duty and move on, helping each child learn grade-level skills as best one can. New teachers appreciate the guidelines. The public is left in the dark on this change and—understandably confused and or hostile—oppose Common Core Standards, simply because it's a change and different. Parents of higher-achieving students worry their children will not get as good an education as in the past. School and district administrators are overwhelmed with state and federal expectations. Politicians, often ignorant—in the sense of not knowing—of what the Standards are and why, hear the complaints and take an anti-Standards view. "Let teachers teach," they argue, blindly hoping to woo their constituents, to speak to those who oppose Common Core State Standards. Teachers' unions may want to maintain the status quo and often resist outside-promoted changes.

No one likes change. No one wants one's long-held belief system shattered. How hard it is to accept that in a new day of technology changing our world that education too must change to better help all students and to provide a brighter future for lower-performing students, the lost students. Who wants to believe that the way school once was must change for a new view of education? Changing a belief system and practice is challenging.

Science historian Thomas Kuhn decades ago delineated a process of change in the scientific community when scientists discover a new theory. It can take generations to win older scientists over to a new theory, Kuhn reports. Some scientists can never let go of the older theory and practice they always knew.

Kuhn's theory sheds light on the difficult process to move to understanding and new expectations in the world of public education. Because of the major change in thinking, understanding, and doing, Kuhn termed this a "paradigm shift."

In education, the old school model isn't working for too many students. A new theory and work must replace the old independence of practice and school emphasis on management versus high-level learning needed for many schools. Once it was generally accepted theory that only "better" students can learn, and these are the chosen few who are best served. Now we know that all students can learn and that we must move out of the egg-carton classroom pattern of teaching to a new way of bringing people together as teams to problem-solve. We need higher levels of learning for all students to meet today's changes in a technology-based world, the inter-dependent global community, a digital world, highly competitive with ever-changing new technology applications, the catalyst for change.

Kuhn reports on the major revolutions in science as being shocking at the time. Such revolutions in thinking—once denigrated—are now well-accepted theories, such as Einstein's theory of relativity, Copernican astronomy, Newton's laws of physics, Roentgen's discovery of the x-ray, and Lavoisier's discovery of oxygen. Roentgen kept seeing a strange blue light in his experiments. The blue light did not conform with accepted thinking in the field. Hence Roentgen's discovery of the x-ray. Theory and practice changed to conform with this discovery. Our blue light in schools is that we are failing too many students. With this persistent observation, we must change thinking and practice. It's hard to accept a new theory of thinking and work. It's earth-shattering for many, simply incomprehensible for others.

Kuhn reports that when new observations see a failure in the traditional theory and practice, the scientific community as a whole begins to recognize that the traditional theory fails to solve basic problems. Schools by their structure of the factory system structure of the 1900s sifted out the poorly performing students. As late as the 1960s—and still in too many schools today—lower-performing students were shunted to low-level classes with limited learning opportunity, and, feeling out of place in school, often left school before graduation. How many do we hear say it was one coach, or one teacher, who kept them out of jail? Now all of school must help. Traditional school hasn't solved the problem of all students learning well. Common Core State Standards put us on this better path.

Some say school isn't broken because many students learn well. But we can do better.

Kuhn states that the core of the crisis is a breakdown of solving problems within the old paradigm. For schools, these are our students who drop out, fight school by becoming behavior problems—often through lack of engagement in class work—do poorly on assignments because they don't know how to do better, and act out their frustration of not being able to learn. A student with no interest in reading the literary classics is brilliant on the athletic field, a dud in the classroom. These problems exist in every school. State standards and tests have brought the learning issue to the forefront. Now we are asked to address this issue, to pay attention, and better help all students.

The new paradigm of focus on learning replaces the bureaucratic school structure of following old rules of conformity. This change is hard to adjust to. With years of experience under the old organization and emphasis on the status quo of management, school people are understandably disoriented—even face a crisis—by the change to emphasize all students learning well. The achievement gap widens with more rigorous tests if school thinking and practice don't change for struggling students. Albert Einstein famously said that the definition of insanity is continuing to do the same thing over and over while expecting different results.

We haven't explained this bigger picture well to the public or to school people. Some veteran teachers see the need for the change to help each child learn at high levels and thus retool and sharpen their skills. But many veteran teachers—those long schooled in the earlier structure and who look to students as categories not capable of improving—may have a hard time accepting the changes to focus on the marginalized "poor" students. Demographics need not be destiny. We haven't effectively presented this case in a way that all teachers can understand the rationale for this tectonic shift to a different way of thinking about school and a different way of working, a different way of serving students who depend upon teachers to learn. Common Core Standards provide the helpful guidance.

Kuhn reports that years of experience under the old paradigm causes difficulty in making a conversion to the new way of thinking. Because scientists are trained to work under one paradigm, the scientist who creates a new paradigm is young or new to the field. Think Steve Jobs, Bill Gates, Mark Zuckerberg. These young men didn't know it couldn't be done.

Kuhn states:

> Almost always the men (sic) who achieve these fundamental inventions of a new paradigm have been either very young or very new to the field whose paradigm they change . . . (O)bviously these are those who, being little committed by prior practice to the traditional rules of normal science, are particularly likely to see that those rules no longer define a playable game and to conceive another set that can replace them (Kuhn, 90).

Those outside the education field who have called for change include state governors.

We take a new look at school. The individual must change to adopt the new paradigm, Kuhn states. State and federal regulations require changes. What's fair for teachers? What's fair for students? Can our schools survive and implement with integrity the new changes? Can the public and the politicians with power to make decisions understand and accept an unpopular and different theory and practice?

Kuhn reports the scientist receives a narrow and rigid education to equip her for puzzle-solving within the tradition the textbooks define. The scientist is not prepared when crises are generated. Kuhn states, "(T)he scientist is not, of course, equally well prepared . . . (S)o long as somebody appears with a new candidate for paradigm, the loss due to rigidity accrues only to the individual" (Kuhn, 166).

Veteran teachers find their long-held beliefs and actions challenged. How can people change a long-held belief system? Not a few teachers retire when new teaching methods and regulations counter and threaten their long-held beliefs and practice. Race to the Top is a seismic culture shift.

How then does change in belief and practice happen?

Kuhn observes:

> The transfer of allegiance from paradigm to paradigm is a conversion experience that cannot be forced. Though some scientists, particularly the older and more experienced ones, may resist indefinitely, most of them can be reached in one way or another. Conversions will occur a few at a time, until, after the last hold-outs are gone, the whole profession will again be practicing under a single, but now different, paradigm (Kuhn, 151,152).

We now have teachers who took state tests as students themselves. For a generation of teachers state tests—once not accepted by teachers but forced by federal policy under No Child Left Behind—are the norm. Standards learning has been part of many newer teachers' own school life. It's not new and shocking for them.

In addition, many veteran teachers intuitively understand this new paradigm. Many experienced teachers take each child under their wing and develop learning. These are our silent saints, who spend time working with individuals, who put their heart and soul into their teaching. They understand their content well and know how to impart this to their students. They're good colleagues. We treasure these teachers. They're known in their school. These teachers live in their students' hearts and minds. We need more such teachers.

A Change in Teacher Evaluation as Part of the New Paradigm

The new Educator Evaluation system under Race to the Top is at its best a fair one, setting out clear areas for proficiency. Four categories are clearly defined. The model is based on mutually agreed areas for growth with one's evaluator. The process is based on "self-directed growth," with the teacher collecting evidence of growth. This can counteract burnout, long an enemy of learning. But teachers wither under a lower-than-expected evaluation of their work. Self-confidence, which we need to do our job well, is shaken. Teachers fear bias in evaluation of their work.

Schools must work harder to support teachers with this dramatic shift. The public must value and help support the high-quality learning that's tested and reported on.

My own old school Hope was once considered a "good" school because a percentage of students went on to elite colleges. However, many—low income and racial minorities—dropped out or were counseled out before graduation. Now those invisible "other" students must be provided a fair shake. A shaky economy, joblessness, jobs loss, technology replacing lower-level jobs—all conspire to build a wall in place of a brighter future for too many students. Kindergarten through grade 12 education needs a makeover.

Another Planet

In adopting a new paradigm, Kuhn states that the scientist must learn to accept new assumptions, rules of behavior, values, and relationships. The world view changes with a paradigm shift.

"When paradigms change, the world itself changes with them . . . what were ducks in the scientist's world before the revolution are rabbits afterward. It is rather as if the professional community had been suddenly transported to another planet where familiar objects are seen in a different light and are joined by unfamiliar ones as well" (Kuhn, 111, 112).

The traditional rules of work that the scientist has been trained to pursue change. He or she must then be helped to see things in a different way, "not as counter-instances, but as different . . . Therefore, at times of a revolution . . . the scientist's perception of his environment must be re-educated—in some familiar situations he must learn to see a new gestalt. After he has done so, his work will seem, here and there, incommensurable with the one inhabited before."

It's a new way of thinking and working. As Common Core Standards are accepted as a framework for learning, all learning improves. We know from research and practice that when teachers focus on Standards learning and effectively engage their students in this learning, this is reflected in strong test scores. Teachers thus gain confidence in their ability and become more effective. We see this in pockets. We have research that shows what can improve student learning. This must happen on a larger stage, a national scale.

Under the new paradigm, "Ducks become rabbits," states Kuhn. The days of the silent classroom are of the past. Now a learning classroom has a feel of energy; students are talking, on task, desks are scattered, the teacher moves around. Differentiation and active learning are now expected. We now are happy when we walk into a classroom where we see students working on varied projects and can't find the teacher, who may be in a corner helping an individual child. Earlier, we expected students sitting quietly in rows with the teacher at the front talking at students. School now looks different, and is measured differently. Teacher collaboration rather than separation is valued; this is stated in the Race to the Top Educator Evaluation guides. We must help one another for this challenge to educate all well. We can still be proud when some of our students move on to MIT, Stanford, or Pomona College. And we can be proud when objective test data reflects our struggling students soaring in learning.

Future Promise, an Act of Faith

A new paradigm is accepted when the community shifts to embrace it, states Kuhn. Individual reasons motivate adoption. Kuhn notes that a convert to the new paradigm must act even in defiance of evidence. What causes conversions to the new paradigm in the absence of hard evidence, when a new paradigm replaces the old one?

There are arguments other than the ability to solve problems that appeal to the individual's sense of the appropriate, notes Kuhn. Will improved assessment results mean higher levels of learning and improve the lives and enhance prospects for our students' futures? This may or may not happen, but it's the best we have today.

This is a national experiment, an act of faith. Do we have a better approach?

The new paradigm, says Kuhn, does not solve all the problems, nor does it convince a community that it can do this. Much study, testing, observation and experimentation is needed to test the fit, Kuhn reports.

We must give the new paradigm a chance. With rival paradigms, the choice, argues Kuhn, must be based on faith.

Kuhn states:

> "(The scientist's) decision must be based less on past achievement than on future promise. The man who embraces a new paradigm at an early stage must often do so in defiance of evidence . . . A decision of that kind can only be made on faith . . . Something must make at least a few scientists feel that the new proposal is on the right track, and sometimes it is only personal and inarticulate considerations that can do that (Kuhn, 158).

How does large-scale professional thinking change? "Paradigm shifts are built more on questions of values than on observable proof . . . the issue is which paradigm should in the future guide research on problems" (Kuhn,

157). Those who pick up the new paradigm and proceed under it then "will develop it to the point where hardheaded arguments can be produced and multiplied." No single argument will persuade all. "Rather than a single group conversion, what occurs is an increasing shift in the distribution of professional allegiance" (Kuhn, 151).

We can't say we didn't see this train coming.

Public education has been slowly moving over 25 years to better serve all students. Most individual states have adopted their own state standards and tests under No Child Left Behind, once widely unpopular, and then accepted as the way of the world for schools. NCLB, once disparaged and barely understood by the public, gradually was, if not embraced, accepted as the norm. People adjusted to state tests and reports, to sanctions on schools with more traditionally underperforming students, and seeing high scores for higher demographic communities. School of the past, for the most part, didn't affect learning ability. Now we face the clear if ugly fact that we haven't addressed the long-term data showing that all students are not as well served in schools as we would like to see. Too many racial minorities, low-income students, special needs students, and English language learners fall too far behind. Tests now look simply for each student's growth each year.

Devoted school education reform leader Deborah Meier, who headed Harlem's Central Park East High School, gained national attention for 100 percent college attendance with low-income and African American students. I asked one of Meier's teachers how she was so remarkably successful in picking up struggling students as late as high school, setting them on their feet, providing fine education, and moving them on to college. "Deborah is persistent," he smiled. "She just talks with you until you get it." The "it" is that we work with students until they learn.

Such beacons of hope as Deborah Meier's school have shown that change can happen. Students can be transformed. School is a new world. Now the next step is simply voluntary state acceptance of more-challenging Common Core State Standards and more-challenging common national tests. If Common Core State Standards were wrong in expectations of students and didn't conform to the best thinking of the discipline, they would not be acceptable. But they conform well with traditional high-level learning standards in the content areas, what we so wish every child could attain. We're ready for this step. We can either jump off or leap onto the train. It's a values issue.

Pieces and supports for the new regulations have long been in place. Ways to assist struggling students are in practice. Many teachers collaborate on learning. Teachers know varied methods of reaching all students that weren't known decades ago. Technology can help us. Teachers study new Standards and test results. Teachers seek help for struggling students. We have the tools.

Do we have the belief system of the new paradigm to guide us through the choppy seas to improve the quality of learning for each student, on a national level? It would be a dream come true.

REFERENCE

Kuhn, T. S. (1970). *The Structure of Scientific Revolutions* (2nd ed.), Chicago: The University of Chicago Press.

About the Author

Many recall the one teacher who changed one's life. Katherine Scheidler learned to love writing, research, and literary analysis of challenging, classic, rich material from two devoted high school English teachers. These teachers pushed students, asked questions rather than lectured, forced their charges to delve deeply into material. These superb teachers set a direction the author couldn't escape. Upon receiving an undergraduate degree from the American University School of International Service in Washington, D.C., Scheidler went on to acquire a fall-back Master of Arts in Teaching English degree at Brown University. Practice teaching at a nearby school sparked a love of teaching and learning, a love of the classroom.

The author taught for several decades in this urban school. She then concurrently served as Brown University clinical professor of Methods of Teaching English and enjoyed supervising Brown seniors and MAT graduate students in their student teaching.

She later obtained graduate degrees from the Harvard University Graduate School of Education and Boston University. As Massachusetts school system Curriculum Director and Assistant Superintendent for Curriculum, Instruction and Assessment, Dr. Scheidler guided the first wave of new State Standards and tests under No Child Left Behind, facilitated and observed increased student learning, and now supports teachers in the next step up with national Standards and tests, taking the fear out of school change through discussion and guidance.

The author's goal is to help all teachers emulate the fine teachers who instill a love of learning and ability to learn at high levels. This is the challenging and exciting work of the path the author has taken, for national excellence in learning, and for each child.

Index

A
ADHD 18
Advanced Placement 5, 28
A Nation at Risk ix, 37

B
back to basics movement 20
Brown University 18, 21, 22
Bush, George H. W. 38
Bush, George W. ix, 38

C
Coalition of Essential Schools 23
Coleman, James 22
collaboration 8, 9, 14, 22, 32, 47, 67, 73
Common Core Standards x, xi, 4, 5, 6, 7, 8, 13, 14, 15, 16, 25, 27, 29, 31, 32, 33, 35, 41, 43, 44, 47, 48, 49, 51, 55, 56, 58, 62, 63, 67, 68, 70, 73
    Anchor Standards for Reading 53
    Anchor Standards for Writing 65
Common Core State Standards iii, ix, x, xi, 3, 7, 8, 9, 13, 14, 16, 24, 30, 33, 34, 37, 38, 41, 46, 48, 57, 61, 62, 65, 68, 69, 75
    Reading standards 50–61
Congress iv, x
criterion-referenced tests 4, 5

D
data 21, 22, 24, 26, 27, 74, 75
demographics x, 10, 18, 21, 22, 39, 70

E
Educational Testing Service (ETS) 6
Educator Evaluation 3, 11, 72, 73
Elementary and Secondary School Improvement Act 37
English language arts 42, 46, 47
English language learners x, 3, 10, 12, 13, 21, 75

G
Governors Summit on Education 38
Graduate Record Exam (GRE) 5

H
higher-achieving students 5, 15, 16, 22, 26, 48, 49, 50, 52, 56, 58, 62, 64, 67, 68
history 15, 30, 33, 54
Hope High School 17–24, 72

I
IQ tests 4

J
Japan ix

K
Kohlberg, Lawrence 60
Kuhn, Thomas 68–74

L
learning disabilities 12
"lone ranger" teachers 8

M
math 5, 6, 9, 12, 24, 25, 26
Meier, Deborah 75

N
National Commission on Excellence in Education ix, 37
National Council of Teachers of English 38
National Council of Teachers of Mathematics 38
National Governors Association x
National Governors Conference ix
National History Day 30
National Writing Project 64
No Child Left Behind (NCLB) ix, x, 7, 12, 24, 38, 72, 75

O
Oakes, Jeannie 21
Obama x, 37, 38

P
paradigm shift 10, 11, 14, 68, 73
phonics 44, 45
Proficient level ix, x, 9, 12, 13, 38, 65

R
Race to the Top x, 3, 37, 38, 39, 71, 72, 73
Reading and Writing Standards 14, 16, 29, 34
    Common Core Anchor Standards 53, 65
    reading 41–49, 50–61
    writing 62–66
reading development 41–49
research skills 14, 15, 25, 26, 29, 30, 31, 32, 33, 34, 35, 54, 62, 64, 65, 66

S
Scholastic Aptitude Test (SAT) 5, 6, 7, 10
science 15, 33, 42, 54, 63, 69
Sizer, Ted 10, 21, 22, 23, 24
social studies 15, 22, 35, 42
special education x, 12, 13, 45, 47
special needs students 3, 9, 12, 13, 21, 45, 47, 75
standardized testing 4
Standards learning xi, 3, 9, 11, 16, 26, 27, 29, 32, 39, 42, 43, 48, 54, 56, 67, 72, 73
struggling students 5, 11, 14, 15, 21, 22, 27, 38, 39, 43, 44, 45, 46, 47, 48, 57, 58, 62, 67, 70, 74, 75, 76

T
technology 28–36
tracking 19, 20, 22
21st Century Skills Initiative 29, 30, 33

U
underperforming students 10, 13, 38, 39, 67, 69, 75
U.S. Department of Education 3

V
vocabulary 6, 7, 25, 42, 52, 56, 60

W
Wilson reading program 45